I0210548

Practical Money Making-
Surviving Recessions, Layoffs,
Credit Problems, Generating Passive Income Streams, Working
Full Time
Or Part Time and Retirement
By
Kim Isaac Greenblatt

Kim Greenblatt Publisher
Published In West Hills, California

Practical Money Making-Surviving Recessions, Layoffs, Credit Problems, Generating Passive Income Streams, Working Full Time Or Part Time and Retirement
By Kim Isaac Greenblatt

All rights reserved. No part of this book shall be reproduced, stored in a retrieval system, or transmitted by any means, electronic, mechanical, photocopying, recording, or otherwise, without written permission from the publisher. No patent liability is assumed with respect to the use of the information contained herein. Although every precaution has been taken in the preparation of this book, the publisher and author assume no responsibility for errors or omissions. Neither is any liability assumed for damages resulting from the use of information contained herein.

The author and publisher specifically disclaim any responsibility for any liability, loss or risk, personal or otherwise, which is incurred as a consequence, directly or indirectly, of the use and application of any of the contents of this book.

Disclosure: The information given in this book is given for the purpose of education. Use any advice or suggestions at your own risk. The author or publisher is not responsible how you manage your life or finances. Please do your own due diligence and use common sense in investing and handling your money. Financial situations are different for each person. What may work for some people may not work for others. Please do your own research.

Good luck!

Copyright 2008 Kim Greenblatt.

Published by Kim Greenblatt,
West Hills, California, United States of America.

ISBN-13 978-1-60622-001-6
ISBN-10 1-60622-001-2
August 2008

This book is dedicated to all of us, my dear readers. We are all in the same boat. We might as well all be paddling in the same direction.

4

TABLE OF CONTENTS

Introduction

Welcome! If you are reading this book you have an interest in money. Maybe you have lost your job, are in debt, have credit problems, or are having a lousy retirement.

Let's see what we can do about changing your life around. My name is Kim Isaac Greenblatt. I am what you might call a multitasker. I have been working multiple jobs for years and like you, have been in and out of debt. I have tried waiting to win the various state lotteries but that doesn't seem to be in the cards for me.

I have suffered through spirit crushing layoffs. I have a family to support including a daughter who has Rett Syndrome. A girl is born with Rett Syndrome every fifteen minutes. Boys born with the Rett gene die at birth.

I get where you are coming from. Each of you is coming from a different place in the financial spectrum and some of the items that I am talking about may or may not apply to you. You may need to refer back to some of these things later on. You may not need to come back to some of the things.

That being said, hopefully there is something in here for everybody! This book is a consolidation of techniques and strategies that have worked for me over the years and hopefully will help you. I am making it. If I can make it, so can you. It will take work and you will need patience but it will happen. If you can find the energy in yourself to read this book, you have taken the first step towards changing your life around.

Congratulations! Please feel free to pat yourself on the back. It doesn't cost a thing! Let's get started.

Kim Isaac Greenblatt
June 10 2008

What Is Your Financial Goal?

Wherever you are financially now, it is important that you remind yourself of where you want to be.

Do you want to be debt free?

Do you want to have enough money to take fantastic vacation trips?

Do you want to own your house free and clear?

Do you want to leave money for your relatives so that they will have a better quality of life?

You don't have to answer the questions for me. You should know the answers yourself and if need be, keep notes and posters of your goals in your kitchen, office or bedroom so that you will have constant reinforcement for what you are doing this for.

It will not be easy. It will not happen overnight. But if you stick to your goals and work at them you will be moving closer to what you have set your heart on.

This is a law of the universe. If you are applying energy in trying to get what you want, you will move towards getting it. There is no magic to it. The biggest problem is – You.

You need to be willing to stay focused and remember what the goal is that you are striving for.

No matter what situation you are in now, you have it within yourself to make the choice to try and improve yourself.

You can do it. If you set your mind to it, you will do it!

Let's deal with some specific blocks towards your financial progress that might need to be addressed.

No Job

You may have been laid off. Maybe you have quit an
intolerable position. The important thing to do is to start
working on a plan to get you back in some sort of position
where you can get an income stream going.

First, if you have been recently laid off, take an inventory of
what you have coming to you. Are you still getting some
severance? Can you bridge your medical benefits over? Did
you make sure that your retirement account, your 401K or
pension plan is secure until you can take some time to decide
what to do with it?

Make sure that they are not cashing out your 401K. If they
are, make sure that you roll it over into an IRA – you will have
generally up to 60 days to do it. If you don't it will be
considered an early disbursement and you will be penalized
and taxed.

If you have been laid off you will have to endure an exit
interview. I wouldn't waste time saying what was wrong with
the company, etc. You will need to use them as a reference. It
doesn't pay to burn any bridges.

By the way, I wouldn't worry about any bad references. A lot
of people are getting laid off and it is sadly pretty
commonplace. Usually by law, a reference check will be that
you worked for the company, were employed there for however
many years and that is that. For personal references pick
people you can trust – you don't want any nasty surprises
when a prospective employer asks "Would you work with this
person again?"

You also will be in a state of shock. Different people deal with
stress differently but there will be some shock whether you are

aware of it or not. It may hit you right away, it may not. However you react is normal.

Getting angry or upset is normal but you shouldn't dwell on those negative feelings. So if you start throwing things around the house and breaking your TV, go for a walk or better yet run and get some of that anger out of your system.

If you need to contact a psychologist, counselor or there is one offered as part of your severance package – take the opportunity. It will help you get back on your feet faster.

Take an inventory of your financial assets and liabilities. If you have a financial savings that isn't in a retirement account, more power to you! You are ahead of most people. That means you have some time and leeway in trying to plan your next step.

If you can, file for your unemployment as soon as possible. The reason I say that is that it takes time for unemployment to process your application (they get a lot of them) and it may be several weeks till you get your first check. It doesn't hurt to get the ball rolling. For the interim, if you have a family, plan on making some cut backs (if you can). Are there things you can start eliminating that you can always do later on?

For example, if you buy a lot of fast food, consider going out to eat only once or twice a week and load up on frozen food or fresh fruit and vegetables. I know that fast food sometimes seems cheaper and easier but in the long run it will only make you fatter and cost you money.

Buy coffee or tea to make at home instead of going to Starbucks. Start drinking generic sodas instead of Coke or Pepsi. Better yet cut out junk food altogether and get on a lean and mean diet for you and your family if you can.

Get your attitude focused on getting a new job. Personally, I don't like waiting to "get it together". If I know the direction I want to go, in this case, getting a new job, I start researching the internet, calling friends, calling relatives, doing whatever I can to get employed. I have a family to feed. You may too!

If you have the luxury of time and money, you may want to use this as an opportunity to change careers. Make sure you understand though that the starting salary of your new career may be substantially lower than what you were use to making.

Make sure that it you have talked it over with your spouse, significant other or loved ones.   If it involves a significant lifestyle change for the whole family, they need to be in on it.

Speaking of lifestyle changes, do you have any services that you don't need while you are laid off? Maybe you need to cancel cable or satellite for a few weeks or months to save some money. Better to pay the rent or mortgage than to be watching the basketball game on satellite in the alley off of the street.

You want to try and get employed as soon as possible. Set some realistic time lines and if worse comes to worse, take some job – any job – that will start bringing some income in. I am not saying you should get a minimum wage job if it will end up exhausting you and you will still be losing money each month. I am saying that you need to be practical.

If you have been laid off for awhile – get your edge back! You need to get back to work and the longer you are sitting around the harder it is getting back to work. Right?

So, you want to keep busy and avoid being lazy.

I would spend 8-10 hours a day working on resumes, calling companies, going to job fairs. I would do whatever it would take.

If you don't have web access, get it. Look for free web access (though I wouldn't send any personal information from a free site personally) at your local library, internet hot zones or neighbor's house (one you can trust). There are tons of ways to keep busy and you will need to write great cover letters and great resumes to get noticed in the crowd. I suggest you keep calling friends as well as head hunters. In fact, try to stay in contact with whoever you think can help you land a job.

Start a website or a blog about what you are doing or what you want to do. Become an authority in your field and you might be pleasantly surprised if what you are saying strikes a chord with people or is unique. If you hustle, your downtime between jobs will be small and you will be employed in no time.

Please check search engines like Google and search on "job postings". As of the writing of this book, there are sites like dice, monster, and craigslist that have postings every day in all sorts of jobs.

Take advantage of this and dive in. It will also keep you busy and sharp. I keep thinking of when my wife Sharren and I would take Jacob (my son) on auditions for acting. You need to be ready and be prepared for a lot of rejection. Get a thick skin.

Keep your suit or dress pressed and ready. In case you get a call that you need to be at an interview right away – you can go in.

If you are over 50 (heck if you are over 35) and have gray hair, feel free to color it. Wear clothing that shows that you are the person ready to go to work and hit the ground running. This is a good idea regardless of whether you are a male or a female.

Show that you are a professional. Get to the interview early so they will see that you are responsible. It might be the one thing that will help you get the job. Let us now move out of survival mode briefly into more practical money making ideas.

Your Day Job

This section assumes that you are gainfully employed. Are you doing all you can to save money with what you are making now?

First the basics, are you able to max out what you are contributing to your 401K or retirement plan at work? Do they match a percentage of the funds that you put in?

Do you have the medical coverage that you need for your family and friends in place?

Make sure your basic survival needs (food, clothing and shelter) are covered.

Make sure you are on track to advance in your career or at the very least, hang onto your job while you either look for another one wait for the economy to get better (whatever that means). Now, if your day job isn't the place you want to be but you are there anyways, do yourself a favor.

Don't tell people how much you hate it there and that you can't wait to leave.

You might get your wish pretty quickly if they decide to start laying people off.

If you are happy where you are at, don't look at the company through rose colored glasses. Take a brutal look at what their future looks like. In this day and age it is not uncommon for companies that were profitable a year ago to be one quarter away from bankruptcy a year later.

If you work for a publically traded company, analyze the balance sheets, the annual reports. If it is a privately owned company, make friends with somebody in accounting and ask them what is going on.

You should still expect the unexpected no matter what you find out. We are living in times of change. Nothing lasts forever.

There is very little loyalty between employers and employees if there isn't money being made. Even if money is being made, if a company thinks they can make more by outsourcing your position, you may be gone.

So start asking yourself some important questions. You need to know the answers to them:

1. Am I happy doing this job?
2. If not, what do I want to do?
3. Can I make a living doing it?
4. How can I move into that dream job without starving myself (or worse, my family) to death?
5. Am I just working to pay for my hobbies, things that I love to do and they just can't be done for free or inexpensively?
6. What can I do to cut down on my cash burn so I am actually in a position to save some money, or if I am already saving money, save more of it?

I will revisit this again because it is so important:

Things are not the way they use to be. Do not assume that your day job is safe no matter what you do for a living. Even city workers who generally have what others might think as a secure job are subject to layoffs if there are budget cuts throughout the city.

If you are in a business market that is in a deep down cycle, like the financial markets in the early 2000s, as of the writing of this book, you may be experiencing some of the bill payment squeezing that you will need to have cash for.

Your 2nd Job

Maybe you are at a point in your life where you are working one job, taking care of a family, maybe going to college or trade school at night. Maybe you need some extra cash. Think about taking a second job.

It doesn't have to be the job of your dreams. It would be great if the job works out to be something that will help you on your dreams or career path. If it is something to just make you some extra money that is all you need.

What are some second jobs that you can take that will make you some money?

Some initial places to look are department stores for seasonal work at stores such as Target, Wal-Mart (if they all haven't gone out of business as of the printing of this book). Maybe your local supermarkets are hiring. If you are looking for discounts to help out at the holidays or if you are a technophile, think of stores like Best Buy, Fry's Electronics or whatever electronics chain store is nearby.

I've worked retail and the skills you need for that are honesty (they test you for your integrity), patience, and the ability to deal with all kinds of people.

The reason turnover is so huge in retail is because most people have no clue how to give good customer service let alone how to react when they receive it. Most people I see working part time act like they are doing the customer a favor.

Please.

Whenever I get service people like that I take comfort that they won't last long at their job.

Make it a point to kill your customers with great customer service. It will help you keep your job longer and people may offer to steal you away at a higher salary!

Good with numbers? How about you think about doing bookkeeping or taxes part time? If you are good with packaged computer tax programs you can work part time helping people do their finances, their taxes, their bookkeeping.

Certification for tax preparation varies from state to state. Make sure that you know what you are doing since you are dealing with people's lives. You might be able to parlay your part time bookkeeping or tax service into something full time after a few years of great service and word of mouth referrals.

WHEN IT MAKES SENSE TO AVOID A SECOND JOB

This may seem obvious but it bears stating. There are situations where you might not want to take a second job.

If you end up having to spend the money you are making on gasoline to drive to your new job, don't take it.

If you will need to spend all that you are making on babysitters, don't take it.

If you end up spending more money as a result of taking the new job and there is no way to recapture the money spent, it is not worth taking the job.

If it throws you into a higher tax bracket that eats up the money you have made, it isn't worth it.

Here is an example that I have seen all too often. A husband works and his wife wants to work part time. Her income throws the couple into a higher tax bracket and they end up paying out what she made plus extra money!

Prior to making a decision like that talk to your tax advisor

WHEN IT MAKES SENSE TO TAKE THE SECOND JOB:

You need the extra money to pay bills, back taxes, boost savings, or lower your mortgage.

You are taking the job to transition into another career and you need to take a low level or entry level position to get into the business you want.

The key reason for taking a second job is help you accomplish your financial and life goals. It shouldn't be an end unto itself.

Seasonal positions that you might look into are day care workers, babysitting, service industry jobs ranging from busboys through hosts or hostesses in restaurants.

What are some other vocations? How about sales, sales and more sales? As holidays come and go, the department stores look to fill in part time jobs with people to help out. As stated before they are looking for honest, bright, outgoing and trustworthy people who they can trust with inventory, their cash registers and their customers.

Fast food restaurants are almost always looking for employees at one time of the year or another.

Do you like to work outdoors and have the physical stamina for the heat or cold? You may want to start or work for somebody with a landscaping business. More and more people want somebody else to mow their lawn when they are dead tired after working a week at work.

On the other hand, for cost savings, in bad times, one of the first things to go is the gardener so you need to look into your local market yourself and see if this is the right position for you.

How about a dream part time or contract job testing video games? You need to be able to communicate verbally and in writing and be able to go over and over the same maps or levels in games to debug problems and let the developers and programmers know what is wrong. Debugging games (hey, debugging software) is a lost art.

With more and more pressure to hit deadlines for shipping, delivering or placing on the internet software products, more and more products tend to get shipped when they should have spent more time being debugged.

If you can do a great job as a tester or debugger, the chances are that the company will do what it can to keep you happy and if full time positions open up, they will keep you in mind.

If you are looking for outdoor positions like lifeguards or camp assistants, remember that you may need to have training and certification as a lifeguard, CPR, First Aid, and you may want to make sure that wherever you are working carries enough liability insurance.

Different surveys suggest that you market to the rich because even in down business cycles they still will have money. If you are trustworthy, you may be able to become a "gopher" for a successful celebrity – that is you "go for this, go for that". Just make sure that the celebrity that you are working for has money. A lot of celebrities have worse financial problems than you or I can imagine and a lot of it is of their own making.

These are just some ideas. Start making a list and burrowing around to see what it is you can find and do!

My Comic Book Delivery Business

Back in the day, one of the businesses that I had part time was a comic book delivery business. At the time, the comic book distributors would sell to anybody who would be able to meet their requirements of ordering retail a minimum of $600 a month.

The first thing that I did when I approached the business was to determine:

1. Can I sell $600 worth of comic books, cards, pogs, posters, books or collectibles a month?
2. What are the licensing requirements for doing business in Los Angeles and California?
3. What are the time constraints for doing this job part time while I work as a programmer analyst and possibly on call 24/7?
4. What is my exit strategy for leaving the business?

Back in the 1980s, comic books were hot as something to be sold as a collectible. There were a lot of independent comics coming out and everybody was buying and selling comics and treating them as if they were stock market commodity items.

I wanted to get into the business because I was familiar with it. I had been collecting comics on and off since I was five years old and I had bought and sold various comic collections. I wanted to be able to get comic books for myself inexpensively and to make some extra money from my business.

I felt that nobody had a delivery service niche for comic books. Would somebody be willing to pay a premium or at least could I get by with minimal discounting for the ability to have your latest books delivered to your doorstep once a week?

Remember, this is before the internet and a lot of inexpensive overnight delivery services.

Here is how I answered and resolved my questions:

1. Can I sell $600 worth of comic books, cards, pogs, posters, books or collectibles a month?

I developed a business plan where I would plan on growing by setting up comic book tables at swap meets and selling product there. I would use that as a place to develop contacts for the comic book delivery service. At the time there were three places for swap meets in the San Fernando Valley and I would go to Orange County to develop contacts as well. I avoided the Los Angeles Comic Book Convention because I calculated that I could not compete with the deep discounting that some people were offering. They eventually went out of business anyways.

I had quite a collection of books and would not mind selling some of the books to generate income.

I figured that with a wholesale discount of 40% - 50% I could easily purchase $300 worth of comics, etc and if worse comes to worse, I would end up keeping the books or try to sell them at the swap meets to recover my money.

If business would take off, I would think about opening a store, getting workers to help me out, etc. If business would be bad, I could close up shop with relatively little exposure.

I did not want to jump into signing a lease and being stuck in a store if I was going to end up losing money.

2. What are the licensing requirements for doing business in Los Angeles and California?

I needed a resale license since I would be buying wholesale and selling retail and I would need a L.A. business license.

Cost for the city license was nominal. The resale license was available from the State of California.

    3. What are the time constraints for doing this job part time while I work as a programmer analyst and possibly on call 24/7?

Sharren, my wife was cool with me working on weekends at the swap meets. Generally it would either be a Saturday or Sunday so I wouldn't be gone both days. Comic books were delivered to the warehouse in Los Angeles centrally on Thursdays and I would plan on picking up my books, sorting them and delivering them that night. I figured I could deliver them all in one or two days.

If business would get better, I would hire some people to deliver books for me.

    4. What is my exit strategy for leaving the business?

At the time, Diamond, the distributor, required that you pay off any outstanding book orders before closing an account. Since I didn't have a lease for a store, I calculated that if I needed to get out of business, I would only be on the hook for two months worth of books.

In keeping start up costs down and looking at what my exit strategy would be, I agonized about what I needed to start the comic book delivery service.

I had saved money and was ready to buy a cash register for a swap meet, a credit card acceptance machine and the wiring for it, stock up an inventory of every comic book, poster and pog I could think of. After calming down and realizing that I would go broke in trying to get everything - not to mention to pay monthly fees for the credit card processing service AND a service charge for each transaction, I settled on the following:

1. Preorder of comic books of about $600 of merchandise, trading cards and posters at the retail level so my initial cost with a 50% discount (if it was that high) would be $300.
2. Licenses for selling comic books and working swap meets (my initial source of looking for clients who wanted me to deliver comic books to) - free.
3. Site fees to set up at each week at either Pierce College or the old Winnetka Drive-In swap meets - $10-20 a week for a table so in a month maybe $80.
4. A cash register - $250.

I mentioned this to a family friend and he said, "Why do you need a cash register? What's wrong with a metal box or even a cigar box?"

He was right! I ended up saving another $250 which I could turn into trading cards which I ended up selling.

I ended up getting clients from the swap meets. Unlike a lot of other people who had jumped into the comic book business to make money, I did not go broke from over-spending with my start-up costs.

In your business, do you really need a plush office? Is image important to what you are selling? If you are an attorney or in marketing, you might need something for potential clients to see that you are serious. You don't have to go overboard like some Century City (a fairly high rent part of Los Angeles) attorneys use to and have marble flown in from Italy and placed in your building!

Think of ways to start up or continue your business that don't cost money. Be creative. There are plenty of one dollar, 99 cents and inexpensive stores where you can find goods to fill the gap that expensive stores sell. A lot of times the products are the same and you are just paying more for the name recognition from buying it from that particular store.

Little things like that may sound cheap but if you are starting up from scratch, trying to take care of a family of four, have a special needs daughter or any or all of the above, you want to make every penny count. It will pay off down the line as well because other business people will respect you for watching your money. Potential investors will see that you can be trusted with money and won't blow it all for things that won't help your business.

Another important point: Nothing beats natural "word of mouth" advertising. The internet allows people to voice their opinion and tell you about goods and services. Sometimes some of the feedback systems can be manipulated but if you read between the lines, take the time to e-mail people or just ask your friends, you will see that honesty in business is rewarded with repeat business!

If you make a good product or offer a good service, people will come back (if they have the money). Not only is it a great and profitable idea (like the great and powerful Oz?), it will happen without you spending a cent (or euro, etc)!

For my comic book delivery service, I went ahead, got permission at college bookstores and placed fliers with my phone number. While I am talking about fliers, do you know the success rate for fliers and hand outs? If you get a 1% return on them you have done great! That means for every 1000 fliers you post or hand out you will be lucky if you get 10 people who will call or e-mail you.

The same problem occurs with web sales. People will tell you "get a web site and drive traffic to it and you will get sales". That isn't always true. You can get great web traffic if you have links showing something scandalous or something exciting.

The problem is that traffic like that is short lived and doesn't translate to sales. It won't help you to get thousands of visitors if none of them actually buy the goods or services that you are selling.

Back the comic delivery business. It took me about three to six months to build up my book of business. An important thing to note is that I watched what I was ordering and didn't buy into the sales pitching of the comic book publishers or distributors and over order non-returnable product.

Keep that in mind with whatever you decide to do if it pertains to sales. Nobody has ever gone broke selling out everything they had in stock.

A classic example of this was a hot comic book like "The Death of Superman" or some comic book "event" happened. People would load up on the comic hoping that it would become valuable and a collector's item.

It did, but for all the wrong reasons. The reason that the comic book took off in sales was that DC Publishing did not anticipate the demand and did not have a large enough first print run. There were genuine limited editions and those were going for several hundred dollars each.

Warner Publications took note of this as the media picked up on the event and chastised the editorial and managerial staff for DC not printing enough books. That was rectified with the "Return of Superman" and they overprinted the book.

As a comic book retailer, I ordered just what I thought I could sell and a few extra books to have around. The reason was that I had heard horror stories from other comic book store owners about trying to unload extra books that they had over ordered.

So, the take-away lesson for the potential business owner is to watch your inventory and order what you think you can sell.

With web ordering these days, it should not be as much of a problem with the exception of the supply chain falling apart and your customers getting mad that their product didn't ship when you told them it would.

Missed ship dates were (and still are) a major problem in the comic book business. Solicitations (orders for comic books) are conducted two months in advance. Problems can happen anywhere in the supply chain from the author or artist being too drunk to finish his book, the editor failing to review a completed book to the printer accidentally printing half the book in Pig Latin.

Each business will have its own unique set of supply chain problems. Make sure that you talk to people in the business or prepare for it so you will know how to deal with irate customers.

The one thing with comic book readers was that they got use to the fact that books were late. Some comic book artists wait years between completing books and if they are hardcore fans they gut it out.

Most customers for other products aren't that forgiving. If you are waiting at a drive up window at a fast food restaurant, every minute seems like a week if you have a carload of screaming, hungry kids.

I would take advantage of any free or super discounted comics to use as free marketing.

People love free.

If you give them a free comic book, a free pog, a free massage, a free car wash, they will remember it. You want them to keep that in mind so when they have money they will think of you and your business.

One of the things that I liked about the comic book delivery business was that other than making a commitment to order a specific number of books each month – that was it. There was no mandatory ordering of marketing materials, no contracts where you promise to get 4 people a month to join in your financial pyramid.

Beware of most multi level marketing schemes or pyramid scams. They don't work. Eventually, if growth goes as exponentially as the home company promises, every man, woman and child on the planet should have one of your products or be working for you.

In the late 1990s and early 2000s that was the promise of cell phone technology. Yes, the use of cell phones exploded. The double and triple digit growth that companies like Nokia and Qualcomm had were expected as the norm and not the exception due to the introduction and acceptance of cheaper technologies. Business analysts made wild hair up their butt predictions that the company was going to double and triple again and again. People got caught up into the hype and like anything else, poured in their money. Those who got in first and took their money out in time managed to do well, others, like in the home purchasing boom that recently busted may have lost it all.

One of the rules that I learned from the comic book business was, "a buck is a buck". If I made $10 profit and others may have made $100 on the sale of Iron Man #2, I didn't hit myself on the head for selling something too cheap. I thanked my lucky stars that I got out of having an inventory of unsold crap. If I could raise my prices and the market would accept them, I would do it. I also tried not to gouge my customers because I wanted them to come back.

Non-Profit Jobs

One of the ways you can get into the position you want is try to do the job for free.

If you wanted to be a tax preparer, there are programs offered through different universities where you will be trained in basic tax preparation in return for volunteering for free for the tax season.

That is a great way to get work experience.

If you are a mediator there are dozens of programs at different levels of government where they are dying to have mediators to handle their backlog of cases that require mediation. You may not get paid but the experience you will get can be added to a resume and give you a leg up against your competitors.

If you are a writer, you may want to volunteer to do the articles for the web pages or newsletters for your local chapters of whatever children's sports group you volunteer for. Is there a senior citizen center nearby? Do they need somebody to offer classes on computer use? Here is your chance to become an educator if that is what you want to do.

If you love working with children and have a large heart, there are thousands of special needs children and adults who need helpers, companions and just somebody to treat them as a friend.

The experience you get doing that is priceless and in some cases you may be able to get special training inexpensively or possibly for free.

Make sure you take any required courses like CPR, basic first aid or whatever certification you need so you will be in compliance with local, State or Federal laws.

While I am on the subject, you may want to research what the licensing and bonding requirements are for any business, including a non-profit one.

Non-profit agencies should offer some sort of reimbursement program if you take courses like CPR. Some companies may reimburse you for specific training. One example is being a floor warden for a large company. The floor warden may be required to know what to do in an earthquake, flood or fire. There may be specialized courses and seminars that you will be required to attend.

Skills like that are great to have in case of an emergency on the job or off!

Generally after a natural disaster they turn to the experts for advice on what to prepare for in case the disaster happens again. Sometimes the companies get lax in their preparations until the next earthquake, flood or fire...

Don't Take On A Job Where You Sell Something That You Love To Collect

The chapter title probably should be "Don't Take On A Job Where You Sell Something That You Love To Collect Unless You Remind Yourself That You Are In Business To Make Money and Not Collect Tsotkes".

One of the great side benefits for being in a comic book delivery business was that I got to buy my books inexpensively. I did not go nuts though on purchasing more and more books because I was in it for the money.

As I worked longer and longer in comic book sales I was finding myself getting more and more business oriented in my decisions and I started collecting less and less. I found that being immersed in comic books as a business didn't so much as kill the hobby for me as sober me up.

Please don't get me wrong, this may have the opposite effect on you. I am just warning you because I don't want you ordering Avon, Jafra stun guns or throwing candle parties and finding out three months later that you are your best customer.

You can't afford to stock up on everything unless that is specifically in your business model. If that is the case, you better have a huge warehouse, a lot of money and you probably don't need me to give you business advice. If you have a warehouse and a lot of money you could teach me a trick or two!

For most of us mere humans, it takes will power to do as the mystics say, "Don't stop and smell the flowers on the path to enlightenment."

The same goes true for taking a part time job at some place that you like. To be fair, it will save you money if you can get the store discount if you were going to buy products from them anyways. You also will be drawing a paycheck from them so that makes sense financially.

When I worked part time for Target Department stores for one holiday season I think I made $1500. I looked at my credit card bills at the time and with my Target discount and special last minute in-store specials spent something like $2600. I think I received more than $2600 worth of goods but it made me realize that maybe it wasn't such a great part time job for me at that time.

Keep these things in mind when looking for part time work or a second job.

A great place to look for work if you have the skills is in the infrastructure trade. Our bridges, streets, dams, networks, buildings are always in need of repairs.

I would hope that in the United States that Congress and our next President pass laws that will generate work at rebuilding our nation's highways. We suffer gridlock in a lot of our major cities. The levies in the South are falling apart and are in dire need of being rebuilt.

Streets throughout the United States are cracked and broken due to wear and tear. People can be put to work and paid doing something useful.

It isn't like these people will take all their money and leave the country – at least, not yet.

Even though the housing trade is hurting throughout the United States as of the printing of this book, skyscrapers are still being built. Hotels and freeways are still being built. Dams and waterways are still being built.

People will be needed to construct these structures.

Are you an out of work chef or cook? How about going down to the nearest adult education facility and start teaching a night class on cooking? Have a specialty like Italian food? How about Japanese cuisine? You can keep your chops and build a reputation as a chef through word of mouth with your students.

Whatever it is you do, you need to brag about yourself. You do this by getting referrals, endorsements and you put them up on your website.   Don't expect to get a lot of web traffic at first (or at all). The website has replaced the business card and paper portfolio as the de facto place to learn about a person.

People today are web savvy and most won't spend a lot of time other than drilling down to something they want and they will want it NOW!

They may end up doing a lot of background research before coming to an educated opinion but if you are the only person who offers inflatable bounce land rentals for birthday parties in a 10 mile radius and your website has testimonials that the children have had a great time, the photos show happy parents and nobody has broken their neck on your rentals, the chances are that they will give you the business for that gig.

It can be that simple provided you research your market and are patient.

Blogs honestly are a waste of time.

Everybody picks up everything that everybody says and parrots back to one another. Then they link back to one another. Then they all give each other an "atta boy" (or "atta girl").

I am guilty of this to a certain degree out of necessity. The way you can get around it is to place content on your website. Offer free information or links to places that offer genuine help to people.

Have you ever noticed on the news how they always go to a specific consultant or person to answer questions or give their opinions on everything from celebrity gossip to the stock market?

Have you noticed that they are not the same person?

Television and media outlets are always looking for experts to give their viewers and readers information. Not everybody is an expert on everything. There may be something that you are a specialist on that nobody else has any experience with.

Maybe you can be the next person to be on television when they are looking for that expert!

If you can become the go-to person for a particular niche, you will end up selling whatever product or service that you are offering. You may not sell a lot of them. That depends on how well you deliver the product or service.

But you will sell at least one of them because there is always at least one person in a niche, providing it is not too specialized.

Try it and you may be pleasantly surprised.

I Have No Money and I Need To Do Something Part Time

If you are in a position where you are debt, you need to get another income stream. The facts are that you don't have income to start a second job. You are not in a position other than to work for somebody else.

If you can, try and get an internship in the field you want to work in and try to get a small salary or any kind of money to establish legitimacy in the business.

If you end up working for somebody else, start saving your money or use it to draw down the debts that are keeping you from going after what you really want in life.

Set a realistic plan to pay off any debts you have and make up your mind to get it done. It will happen.

Home Equity Loans (HELOCS) are being frozen as of the printing of this book. You may have been a position to access money from the bank and that money is cut off.

This will be a good time to cut costs, if you can.

Start looking around your neighborhood, on the internet, asking friends what is out there that you might be able to do to make some extra money.

This isn't the time to be bashful.

There are a lot of other people out of work and at least for the interim, it is going to get worse before it gets better. The people who will make it through this will have discipline and will be able to stay solvent.

I have faith in you. If you try, it may not be easy, but you will be able to do it!

Make Money Doing Things That People Hate To Do

You can make money in the meantime trying to do what people hate to do.

When people ask me, "Kim, what is one of the easiest ways to make money?" I have to tell them that there aren't any easy ways of making money short of inheriting it and leaving it to earn simple interest in a safe investment instrument. An easier way to make money though is finding what people hate to do and jumping into that market and doing it.

Take something simple like recycling. Back in the day, nobody wanted to haul or pick up trash. The savvy businessmen and companies that got involved in the trash hauling business discovered there was big money in contracts with other companies and even cities in disposing of garbage. The logical business after that was recycling. Getting people's garbage, sorting out what has monetary value and reselling it seems like a no-brainer during the green, ecological thinking times we are in now but the way to make money in that business is long gone. Simply put, the markets have already been mined, they are fiercely competitive and you would have to find places where it hasn't been worth somebody's business to start a trash collecting business.

The other major problem in finding businesses where people hate to have anything to do with them is that you have to make sure that there isn't a global competitor who can undercut you. Most people don't like to write computer code for example. You would think that computer programming would still pay decently and it does for some markets. If it is an up and coming computer system or product and people haven't jumped all over yet, you may have a couple of years of setting yourself up a decent practice with it. If you do good work and word gets around, you may be able to continue in the market despite saturation as more international outsourcing companies come on board to try and undercut you.

An interesting problem is that like all other products, even outsourcing gets to be expensive or not worth the aggravation if it ends up costing you clients or business. The reason some call centers are back stateside here in the U.S. is that some Americans still give good customer service over the web and phone and actually understand what your issues and concerns are.

So here is what I would do if I were young and looking for a great business move:

I would start looking at what are the junky jobs or things that people don't want to do and how much can I charge for me to do it? Is it also something I can physically (and psychologically) stomach doing even though I may be making money with it.

If you are a sewer electrician, you probably are working for utility companies or cities all the time. Not everybody is cut out for that work and it can be hazardous. Besides accidents happening underground, you can fall, get infection, possibly get electrocuted, well you get the idea.

Do you know why movie producers generally pay so little for new script writers, actors or actresses? It is because they know that there are thousands of people out there who will do that kind of work for free just to have exposure.

You will not find many people wanting to go down into a wet, cold and dark sewer to work on decaying electrical wiring and a rusted junction box for free.

Just remember in your planning to account for taxes and as usual, write your business plan down!

If you can think of any yucky jobs that people don't want to do, let me know. I know there is at least one TV show on cable about it and I suspect there will be more if nothing else just for the shock factor. For a lot of people they can live with the dirt and risk if the price is right.

The question is, is it also right for you?

Remember that start up costs are low when doing a yuck job that nobody wants to do for somebody else and you can eventually move into running your own job later on your own.

If I had to do it over again I would think about being a plumber. Even in times like this when money is tight, there are always people who don't like to get their hands dirty. In some cases, it may not be practical for them to dig up their lawn, root around for their water pipe, look for a leak, try not to hit an electrical line and replace it.

People, like you and I, who are living in a post-industrial culture like their indoor plumbing. We like to be able to go into a room like the kitchen, pull a lever and have water-clean water-dispensed to us. We like to use our toilets inside of the house as well.

When people are having serious plumbing problems, they may balk at the price but they will pay whatever it costs to stop the tree roots from invading their pipes or their laundry water from flooding their house!

If you start thinking along these lines, you will get an idea of some of the jobs that people don't want to do. Be warned that in tough economic times, people will try to learn to do things themselves to save money.

The plus side is that when they mess it up, they have to call in an expert to fix it!

Things You Should Consider When Picking A Business

One of the biggest questions I get asked is, "Kim, what kind of business should I get into? What is the next 'big thing'?"

If I could predict the next big thing I wouldn't be consulting, doing taxes, writing, publishing, managing or coding. I would be doing the next 'big thing'.

The cliché answer is unless you really have an innate ability for correctly guessing the fickle public's taste; don't bother trying to guess what the public wants next unless you have a lot of money to burn. The number one thing you should be looking at is whether or not you like the business you want to get into. It is a lot easier to do something you love than something you hate. Millions of people around the world are doing jobs just to get by. Here is a chance to do the one thing that you love.

You like to design rooms? If you think you can make a living with it in the market you are in, go for it. Bear in mind that you will have to figure out a business plan before you can actually start your business but make sure it is something that you love doing.

You may be pleasantly surprised that your business may turn into the next "big thing" and you will be there waiting to take advantage of it. The number two thing you should consider is what is your realistic income potential?

You may like to design rooms but if everybody else in Trenton, New Jersey or Ankara, Turkey is also interested in designing rooms the chances are that you will have a lot of people offering to design rooms for free. You will have a hard time paying the bills. Keep in mind that jobs (full or part-time) that are glamorous, exciting or fun have a lot of people wanting to do them. Competition is fierce and the market reflects the income you can potentially make accordingly.

If you are starting something brand new, or something yucky (cleaning out people's sewer lines), you will have less people (depending on the market in your area) in competition so you can forecast a better income stream.

Whatever it is that you decide to do, take the time to make a business plan. A business plan is a blueprint for what you are planning to do. It should serve as a written document you can show others, potential bankers or people with money to invest (if you go that route) that you know what you are doing and know the direction that you will be going towards.

Things You Should Consider When Picking A Business Part II

Let's say that you've decided to do the job of your dreams. You really enjoy baking things at home. You think you would make a great baker. Maybe you love to fix things around the house. You've sat down and you have worked out that you think you could make a pretty good living doing this. The next question you need to ask yourself is, how easy is it for me to get started in the business? This is called the ease of entry into the business or initial starting requirements.

You need to know or be able to research what the requirements are for doing business in the particular field that you want to work in. A good place to start is to strike up conversations with people who are doing what you are doing and don't live near your geographical location. If you want to be a plumber, for example, you may want to talk to one that isn't close to you so the person won't feel threatened. In the case of being a plumber, he (or she) probably won't feel threatened because there is a specific path of entry into being a plumber - you need to apprentice with an experienced plumber, take classes, etc.

This is the type of information you need to figure out before getting into your business. Do you have to have any specific licensing requirements for the city, county, state or national level in order to demonstrate competency for what you are planning on doing? You don't want a doctor who has had one year of junior college making a diagnosis on you and it is to be expected that different careers or businesses have different requirements.

If you don't have the requirements now, your mission is to determine what do you need to do to get the skills, how long will it take and will it be worth my while to go through the process to learn the skill or trade or get the street credentials that you might need.

That dovetails nicely into the next factor for consideration:

Is there a market demand for what you want to do?

You very well may want to be a plumber but if there are already ten plumbers in your area and there aren't a lot of people, there may not be a lot of work to go around. On the other hand in a large city like New York, Los Angeles, Chicago, Houston or Miami, you may not have to worry about finding work since there are enough people with broken sinks, toilets and water pipes to go around.

Here is where you take stock of your existing skill sets. If you have always been handy since you were a kid and have read up on how to change pipes, love working with PVC, and already have connections in the industry - you are on your way. The remaining aspect to this would be to demonstrate reliable work habits - are you on time for your jobs, are you honest, do you go the extra mile for your customers, things like that.

If on the other hand you hate working with your hands, hate getting dirty and have a fear of dirty water, maybe plumbing isn't the career choice for you.

Things You Should Consider When Starting a Business Part III

You've found a great job you want to do, you have the knowledge that you can make a living at the job, and there is demand for your skills.

But is your job recession proof?

Are you doing something that withstand the swings that we sometimes encounter (like now for argument's sake) when people's checkbooks close and money is tight? Is the job or product or service you are providing something that people will still pay money for no matter what the economy is?

Consider starting a restaurant. When times are good, people eat out all the time. They would rather pay for the convenience of somebody cooking for them because they are all too tired from working. Let's face it that is what microwave ovens are for as well. People are hungry and what instant gratification N-O-W.

What about when times are tough? The first thing that happens with most people is that they see what they can get rid of in terms of expenses. Where can they cut costs? For a lot of people that means shopping at the Dollar Tree stores and buying $1 meals. Cooking at home means they are saving money and the same goes for starting to bring a bag lunch to work instead of going out and spending anywhere from $7 to $15 for lunch like they use to.

If you are planning though on a business where you can sell inexpensive food, like a hot dog cart in a good location, you may have a recession proof business. Remember you still need to do your own due diligence and planning.

Things You Should Consider When Starting a Business Part IV-
Start Up Costs and Overhead

In your business plan, you need to have what your start up costs are and what your monthly overhead will be for running the business. This would be a good time to also take inventory of your monthly personal expenses because if you are planning eventually on quitting your day job (or making this new gig your new day job) you should know how much you need to live on each month.

Whatever numbers you come up with figure anywhere between 10-35% extra padding should be added to account for emergencies, holiday expenditures and if all things go well, money for expansion of your business.

Let's take the previously mentioned example of a hot dog cart. I have no idea if these numbers are realistic but they are here to serve as an illustration of start up costs:

Hot dog cart	$3000
Hot dogs	$200
Buns	$200
Condiments	$75
Business license	$25
Resale license	$0
Fliers	$100
Sodas and chips	$540
Total Start up Costs:	$4140

And we will throw in 10% emergency cash of $414 to make our total start up costs a grand total of $4554.

Let's say you need to replenish the hot dogs, buns, sodas and chips each month. I know I forgot to add napkins and aluminum foil so I can take some of that money from the emergency cash I allocated up front.

Our monthly overhead might include gasoline to drive to a location, say the front of the County Courthouse at lunch time - $300 a month.

Figure $1015 a month for expenses.

That is your monthly forecast for what you will need in the worse scenario cases if you don't even sell one hot dog. Are these acceptable costs for you and do you have the money to gut it out for 3-6 months till people see your cart and start realizing what a delicious hot dog really tastes like? What if the weather is lousy and you are stuck with rain for three months? How will you make expenses meet in the meantime since hot dogs won't keep forever and you will have to re-buy new ones?

Again, please be sure to do your research in advance and make sure that the startup costs aren't too high or that your expenses aren't going to mushroom out of control and eat up all the profits that you should be making!

Things You Should Consider When Starting A Business Part V-Competition

Let's say that you have all the other elements for your imaginary hot dog cart business planned out. The next thing you need to take into account that should be incorporated into your business plan as well is your competition.

What are you up against in your anticipated marketplace? If you are selling hot dogs outside the city courthouse are there already three other hot dog vendors out there? Are all of them swamped at lunch and it looks like that if they had a dozen hot dog carts that they all would still be swamped?

Just because there is a lot of competition that doesn't mean that you should run away. On the contrary, that could mean that there is a huge demand for the product or service that you are trying to sell. You need to recognize though if the competition is seasonal or timely.

People won't eat dogs (usually) at 7 am in the morning if they are going to work at the courthouse. They might eat though between 11 am and 2 pm throughout the day. Maybe between 4-6 pm you might get another bump in business.

In the toy business, your seasonal sales in the United States are usually from October through December. In India, you can sell gold for weddings generally before monsoon season.

Are you also different enough from the competition to draw business to you from your competitors? Maybe you sell kosher hot dogs. Maybe you have a cute girl in a bikini serving the hot dogs. What is your edge that will differentiate you or your product from your competition?

By recognizing your competition and incorporating it in your business plan, you show potential investors that you know what you are doing or at least have researched your market enough so that they can see that you are taking yourself seriously and will be treating your job as a business!

Things You Should Consider Before Starting a Business Part VI-Time Commitment

Do you like to work long hours? Can you deal well with aggravation and stress? If you are planning on starting your own business you need to be able to deal with working ten to twelve hour work days initially. It will be your business and it will grow or wither away depending on how much time and energy you put in.

If we go back to our hot dog cart example, you can figure that you will move your cart from place to place to try and maximize the amount of hot dogs you can sell in an 8-12 hour period of time.

Let's say you need to open up your hot dog cart at the courthouse at 11 for the lunch hour rush. You are there for two hours so plan on getting an additional two hours of preparation each day to get to your first destination. From 2-4 you travel to some construction sites or to a stadium. From 4:30-6 pm you go back to the courthouse or stay at the stadium. Let us say that you move to an outdoor mall by the ocean to get the late night traffic. You end up staying there till 10 pm. You then take 1-2 hours to go home, clean up the cart and get ready for tomorrow's day.

Ask most independent businessmen and you will find that they work up 10-15 hour days easily. Most of them enjoy what they are doing so initially it isn't a problem.

But if you want to have a social life and get back to your family, girl friend, boy friend or relative of choice, you need for them to understand that initially they won't be seeing much of you because you are trying to start your own business.

Developing Passive Income Streams

One of the ways that you can help make money is by developing passive income streams.

What is a passive income stream? A passive income stream is money that flows to you and you aren't actively doing any work to generate it.

That actually is a misnomer because you do have to do something initially to make a business decision or some action to set up the conditions that you will be generating passive income.

What are some passive income streams?

Royalties from music, book, or movie sales are desirable passive income streams.

Interest or investment income coming in from income such as money coming in from options (such as covered calls, etc.) dividends, etc.

A covered call is where you own stock and you basically sell the right to another person/purchasing entity to buy your stock at a certain price by a certain date. Covered calls are an additional way to generate income streams but have to be researched and are a little out of scope of this book other than to make you aware of them. For more information I recommend that you visit The Chicago Board of Options Exchange:

www.cboe.com

They have some good tutorials for free on how to invest in options.

It is not a good idea to invest in options with bread and egg money. You need to have a strong stomach, do your homework and be patient.

I will go on record stating that if you do your own research and due diligence, you may find some stocks to invest in that will provide you with a decent income stream of covered calls. In the current economic climate, that will take some work and patience.

An example of a covered call would be:

Assume that you are long 100 shares of Kim Corporation currently at $19 a share, and you think that, based on the market slowdown (or whatever reason you want) this stock is going to remain relatively unchanged through July expiration. You could sell one Kim Corporation (shown with whatever symbol it is set for if it were a real Corporation) July 20 Call for 1.75.

This means that you get immediate cash credit of $175.00, with the obligation that if the stock goes up past 20 and the holder exercises the Call, you will deliver your stock at $20 a share.

If this happens, since you sold the Call for 1.75 and would sell the stock for $1 over its present price of $19, you stand to earn a maximum profit of 2.75 if the stock increases past 20.

However, if the stock stands still, remaining at $19 at the July expiration, you get to keep the $175.00. That is Covered Call Selling.

NOTE: If the stock price falls, you are still a stock owner, and are subject to the full loss of your stock investment, reduced only by the $175 credit from the sale of the Call. Also, take it on faith for now but that when you are writing an option on a stock with a low cost basis, there are tax issues to consider upon assignment (when your shares are called away).

Other passive income streams can be generated by creating something that you can resell again and again.

If you are writing music or making movies and selling them, you get paid royalties each time the music or movie is played.

The same holds true for writing and publishing books. In my case, every time a person buys one of my books, I get a portion of the money, a portion goes to cover the print costs, a portion goes to the retailer and I choose to donate a portion of the money to finding a cure for Rett Syndrome.

The upside of this is that I get the money credited to my account whether I am aware of it or not.

The downside is that for any creative venture (and publishing music, videos or books are no exception) – I need to market everything myself. As a self publisher, I am responsible for my content, my deliverables, my business contracts and it takes work.

If you are willing to put in the work that is needed to get out there and you have the drive and patience to generate a product that you think people will pay money for – please go for it!

Don't wait for permission from somebody to do it. The internet and businesses are full of "me too" businesses and that should give you an idea of what sells and what people think will sell.

If you think you have the next "big thing", you will need to take a chance and try to develop it yourself.

What about if you think you may not have the next "big thing" but have something that is commercial, meaning that you think you or someone can make money with your ideas or products?

I would say that it might be easier to get your product accepted.

Here is an interesting question for you:

Do you think publishers (of music, of TV, movies or books) are going to react and publish something brand new and exciting or something that has sold already?

Take a look at what you listen to on the radio, on your iPod, off of the internet. What are the most popular TV shows or movies that people watch?

Despite what they say about looking for something "new and exciting", publishers and distributors are notoriously leery of taking a chance on something that hasn't been proven to generate income.

Notice that the expression you will hear a lot of is "the next big thing". The next big thing isn't always the next original big thing and may not make them money!

That is why when you are making a sales presentation or pitch that they want to know what it can be compared to or what is it similar to.

The classic examples of this are movie ideas – "The movie is like Jaws but set in a space station". "The movie is like Rambo only the lead is a Persian girl who is an Olympic gold medal speed skater!" You get the idea.

Creative business people and artists are given bad advice if they are told that businesses are looking for "new" ideas. The Japanese people made an art form out of taking old ideas and incrementally developing them. The reason China and India rose to financial power in the last thirty to fifty years is simple economics. They were able to compete by providing goods or services cheaper. It remains to be seen if there is anything "new" or "innovative" that will be revolutionizing our lives soon. There has been severe backlash though because a lot of people have realized that because something is cheap, you sometimes get in quality what you paid for!

Getting back to taking and old idea and making it better....

Apple took basically an mp3 player that had been on the market for years, repackaged it and marketed it as the iPod and created a marketing monster.

So if you want to see what is selling in the particular commercial market you are trying for – take a look now at what is selling, see if you can do something similar (only better, or cheaper, or faster or all of that) and try to do it.

Some examples from my own life are that I have found that there is already a niche and commercial market for gambling books. I have made a little bit of money jumping on the wave of the Texas Hold'em craze that swept the world in the last few years. The game is still popular, still on television but the sales for the books and overall interest has flattened.

During this time I thought with the limiting of internet gambling for U.S. citizens that home games would grow in popularity and people would want to learn more about home games like "Crazy Pineapple". Crazy Pineapple is a poker game that use to briefly be played in casinos and is played in home games as well as some casinos, card clubs and some limited poker championships. There wasn't a book on Crazy Pineapple in print. I figured I could create a market.

It didn't happen.

In retrospect, I would now poll my readers, gamblers and websites to see if a book like that would sell. I would start up a website and exclusively make it everything and anything on Crazy Pineapple 8 or better. If I didn't get any response – I wouldn't waste my time with the book.

So how does that affect you?

If you love singing, try recording some songs and put them up for sale through something like one of the iPod sites or through any of the music sharing sites.

If you see that people aren't downloading your song, try giving it away for free and see if people will listen to it and write some positive reviews for you.

A good rule of thumb that I always subscribe to is that if you give something away and people still don't want it that is a great indicator that you have something that people would not pay money for!

You need to go back and re-examine your market, your product or yourself.

Ideally, the best passive income stream is to have ten million U.S. dollars invested in government Treasury bills at 5 percent. Your investment is backed by the security of the U.S. government (well at least for now) and you are getting a guaranteed rate of return. Of course if you had ten million dollars there are other places to put your money safely and to get better rates of return. If you have ten million dollars free and clear to invest let me know so we can add your advice to the next edition of this book since you would sound like you know what you are doing!

Back to how I approach passive income streams.

In my case, I try to get my income stream to grow incrementally but steadily. I try to publish books that I know will at least break even within three months. I try to do 2-3 books a year. I won't get rich overnight on royalties but if I am doing my homework, writing and publishing something commercial, I am building a library of books that I will try and keep in print.

I get paid from sales from my books two months after every sale so basically from when the book is first published till when I get money can be as long as three months. I also may only make a few hundred dollars on the book. That isn't enough to live on but it is enough to help out.

I invest sweat equity. Sweat equity is the time and energy I spend in developing, publishing and marketing my books and getting the websites up that have relevant content.

If you can delegate jobs to people to do and pay them inexpensively or offer them internships by all means go for it. It will allow you to free up your time to do whatever it is you are best at in running your business.

Think For the Future

Most multi-national corporations use to plan for years in the future. The Russians use to publically proclaim in the former Soviet Union their "five year plans". Candidates for the office of the President of the United States always talks about their plans for the next four years when they are running.

I think most businesses these days and people are very shortsighted and you will be very surprised to see anything other than plans going out to the next quarter with the exception of some of the world's largest companies.

Even with change happening literally overnight in industries you need to take that into account and make plans for the future.

What are you planning on retiring on?

What if you get sick or injured and can't work?

What if your industry becomes obsolete?

What if the town I am living in is going under and I can't sell my house?

I am not advocating that you become a worry wart, just, er a practical wart.

I will harp on this in chapter after chapter. You need to save money and make sure that you have enough money to last for at least six months to a year in case something happens.

That money, like any retirement money in an IRA or 401K plan has to be sacred. You cannot touch it.

Circumstances can change literally overnight. Even if you have insurance and you are hit by a flood (as the people in the Midwestern United States as well as people all over the world have been lately) it will take time for the insurance companies to reimburse you, for stretched emergency services to come to your aid so you better be able to access cash to take care of immediate problems like food, clothing and shelter.

The money should be in a checking account (maybe an interest bearing one) or savings account. It should be liquid (meaning you can get to it as cash right away).

That was the doom and gloom side of the chapter. Now here is the sunny and funny side of the chapter.

Make your plans for that retirement in the sun somewhere or for wherever you want to be or do later on. Plan on taking vacation trips to where you are thinking of retiring.

Exploration vacations aren't going to be cheap. You can't get there without money or somebody else paying the tab for your travel expenses. You will need savings for that.

If you realize that all you wanted to do was open up an orchard and grow apple trees, start planning on where you can grow the best apples and where you can get water and land relatively inexpensively.

You are getting the idea. You need to start your planning now and here is a simple yet next to impossible task:

Stick to the plan.

If other events are threatening to break you and you need to get into money to cover expenses – try and fight tooth and nail to protect the money.

If you end up in digging into your money make sure that you can replenish the money (with interest if you can) as soon as you can.

Make sure that your medical insurance and coverage is current. Costs for taking care of you or your loved ones will not be going down in our lifetime from what I can tell. It bears repeating that you don't want your life savings wiped out because of medical bills. Invest in preventive health by watching your diet, exercise and keep a positive attitude towards life.

I realize that is easier said than done but it will add years to your life in terms of your body's health and your checking account's health.

Next to money, and your health – time is the most valuable commodity that you have. That leads to building your nest egg.

Nest Eggs

You may or may not be in a position to be worrying about a nest egg. It could be you are working through paying off debt, have huge medical obligations, or you are already retired.

It is never too late to save money. It may take longer and you may not hit the goal you want but good savings habits are the cornerstone to providing for your future.

You can't count on the government to take care of you. You can't count on relatives (well, maybe you can, but a lot of us aren't in the position to count on them because they are in worse financial shape then we are).

If you are already retired you may be feeling the crunch of having to try and live on small savings or retirement income. You may need to take a part time job so you don't plow through your retirement savings. If that is the case, you need to crunch the numbers if you are receiving social security to see how that will affect your tax situation.

I have done tax returns where retired people have gone back to work to make extra money so they can make their ends meet and they have been nailed with more taxes and less income because they didn't take into effect that their social security would be lowered by the virtue of their working.

Back to nest eggs in general.

Financial planners have come to some pretty interesting realizations over the last few years. Despite great planning, you may be in trouble when you retire depending on when you retire. The traditional advice use to be to have your money in fixed rate of return investments and so-called "safe investments" like bonds, etc.

The problem with this is that inflation, which has been around with us and is going to be biting us very hard now eats up into our buying power.

If you don't believe me, look at the cost of gasoline and food, two commodities that haven't been included as part of the cost of living adjustments for inflation but are the gorillas standing in the room when it comes to watching your money get spent.

Back to the realizations of the investing gurus:

If you retire when the economy is doing well and you are making great returns on your investment under conventional wisdom, you are set.

If you retire with the economy doing poorly and you aren't getting great returns and your portfolio is down, you have problems.

Their solution is to continue to invest in different types of investments even while in retirement. It requires though that you do have savings and it depends on the percentages of the money that you want to allocate for living the rest of your life.

I am not a financial advisor. Please consult with licensed professionals for specific advice. The general advice I am going to give you is that the instead of keeping all your eggs in one financial basket, you need to keep them in two or three baskets as follows:

The theory is that you need to be in a position not to sell off income earning assets to cover your expenses, so you need to divide your investments into three categories:

1. A checking account, hopefully interest bearing that has enough money in it for monthly expenses.
2. An emergency investment account that has roughly two years of living expenses invested in short term securities

and bonds. The purpose for this is to have a guaranteed source of income so you don't have to touch item 3.

3. A long term investment account where you have the bulk of your long term investments and hopefully where your money can have a little bit of risk to grow and stay ahead of inflation.

The theory is that during bad stock market times, the money in the number 2 account should have enough of an income stream so that you don't have to sell stocks during a down period and can wait for the market to recover.

Remember this isn't for everybody and you need to talk to some financial advisors you can trust in order to do this.

Suggestions are for example if you have a nest egg of $1,000,000 (it may seem like it is impossible for you to have this but season to taste percentage-wise based on your own savings).

Let's say you need $45,000- $50,000 to live on. You would need $100,000 in the tier 2 account (that would be roughly two years of what you need to live off) and the $900,000 in the long term portfolio. This way, in case things are bad for the two years, you don't have to touch your long term investments and have enough to live on.

You need to discuss with a certified financial planner what investments would be right to help you plan if you choose this method to try to cover any financial possibility – something that even experts can't do!

There are other investments with insurance and annuities but frankly, a lot of them come with a lot of fees, higher risk versus reward and require a lot of research. Remember that insurance companies normally are investing on the law of averages and they want to stack the deals in their favor. Business is business so buyers beware. They may be right for you. I am not comfortable with them at this point in my life nor do I have large amounts of money to sink into investments I wouldn't be touching for years.

Another weird, unspoken bit of silliness on my part is that I don't want to make it in the best financial interest of an insurance company or corporation for them to have me killed so they can collect my insurance if they had an insurable interest in me and they needed the money.

Silly and paranoid, perhaps, but when it comes to money, especially large amounts of it, it doesn't hurt to be a realist.

That being said, it is a great idea to have term life insurance if you have a family, long term care insurance and disability insurance if you can afford it.

More realistic scenarios are that you might be injured or disabled and not have enough money for medical treatments, mortgage payments or food.

Back to nest egg planning...

The important things that I want you take away from this chapter are that nobody can predict how the economy is going to move and it doesn't hurt to have your money tiered so that even though you are sacrificing some financial growth, you are providing some bit of financial safety for yourself and your family.

Here is another thing you have to worry about:

You don't want to deplete your savings before you die. Statistically if you start withdrawing too much money early on in your retirement, you will run out of money.

Jim Otar, who has a website, retirementoptimizer.com, has different calculators that show that you need to keep your withdraw rates from your investments low. He suggests that if you keep your withdrawal rates at 3.6% or less your first year and keep an investment mix of 40% stocks and 60% bonds, your nest egg would have a success rate of about 100% meaning that it could last indefinitely. Subsequent withdrawals could be adjusted for inflation.

I don't endorse any specific method of investing but I want you to make sober decisions. You will not be able to sustain ten percent withdrawals from your retirement fund and be able to survive financially for more than 19 years. In this case, less is more when it comes to withdrawals.

I do believe that people must adjust their standard of living down in general. When you will be retired, I am not stating that you should go on a diet of cat food and wear potato sacks as clothes (though if it shows that eating cat food and wearing potato sacks would make me immortal I am on board with that).

I am cautioning prudence and the advocating of savings because our health will be declining and all indications are that the cost of living will be going up, not down.

Pay Off Debts Faster

For some of you, this chapter may be one of the most important ones in the book. If you are in debt, your number one priority after food, clothing and shelter is paying off your debt.

Most people carry a lot of debt that will not benefit them. By that I mean credit card debt, debt that you cannot deduct interest on at tax time.

The first thing you need to do is get a grand total of all the debt that you owe and decide the best plan of attack in reducing it.

You may try to call the credit card companies and ask them for a lower rate of interest. They may or may not go along with that. There are two schools of thought with paying off credit card debt:

1. Tackle the big bills that are generating the largest interest payments so you can climb out of the hole faster.

2. Pick the lowest outstanding balance of your credit cards regardless of the interest liability and pay it off so psychologically you can see that you can do it.

Some people advocate consolidation loans. A consolidation loan is a loan where you borrow a lump sum of money to pay off all your credit card debts.

Those can work well providing:

1. You make more than the minimum payments due on the consolidation loans.

2. You don't charge up your credit cards while you are doing this, otherwise you have defeated the purpose of getting the consolidation loan.

Getting back to paying off your credit cards...

You will want to make more than the minimum payments to take care of the debt. It is as simple as that. In order to make a dent into outstanding balances, especially when you get interest added monthly, is to make enough of a payment to lower the balance. When you lower the balance, the interest calculation is on a lower amount so hopefully your next payment will be lower as well.

If interest rates go up, or are looking to go up, look around for other credit cards where you might be able transfer your balance so that you will have less money to pay on interest.

At this point, you probably are asking, "Where will I get the extra money to make the additional payments? I am already stretched thin."

As we touched on earlier, maybe you need to get a part time job. With the holidays approaching cyclically around October – December and with summer break around June-September, you need to remember to apply early (and often) to various jobs to get a part time position.

Be realistic with your payments. If making an extra $200 a month is going to break you, start smaller with an extra $20 a month and build up slowly as your budget gets use to you having to spend more and more of it towards lowering your debt.

You will make a dent and like anything else, the more you practice something, whether it is riding a bicycle, saving money or paying bills, the better you will get at it.

Tear up new credit card offers if you get them in the mail or through the internet. Unless they are offering you deeper interest discounts, there's no reason for going with them. Even if they are offering you deeper short term interest rates, read the fine print. It won't do you any good switching to a lower rate for six months if the interest rate skyrockets after six months.

As I've stated before, but once you get out of the habit of using credit cards, don't fall back in. See if you can adopt a cash only system. I understand that for some people that might be hard to do or impossible.

You can choose to stop receiving "prescreened" offers of credit from companies by calling toll-free:

1-888-567-8688

That phone number is active as of the printing of this book. It is the phone number, that by law, the credit agencies had to establish to allow you an option to opt out of receiving credit offers.

You could also opt out by sending letters to:

Equifax Options
P.O. Box 740123
Atlanta, GA 30374-0123

Experian Target Marketing
P.O. Box 919
Allen, TX 75013
TransUnion Opt Out Request
P.O. Box 505
Woodlyn, PA 19094-0505

Think of every time you have spare change, a yard sale, an unexpected bonus from work or any other financial windfall. Use the money to pay off credit cards.

The same principles can be used for paying down mortgages and home equity loans. Property values come and go in cycles. If you can, go back and renegotiate the terms of your mortgage or your home equity loan to a payment plan and interest rate that can be something that you can work with.

The following section is similar to one from the FTC and deals with cleaning up one's credit. It can be done with patience and planning. If you are in a position where you don't have money to begin with, the last thing you want to try to do is end up spending more money to save money!

Credit Repair: Helping Yourself Out of Bad Credit

You see the advertisements in newspapers, on TV, and on the Internet. You hear them on the radio. You get fliers in the mail. You may even get calls from telemarketers offering credit repair services. They all make the same claims:

- "Credit problems? No problem!"
- "We can erase your bad credit — 100% guaranteed."
- "Create a new credit identity — legally."
- "We can remove bankruptcies, judgments, liens, and bad loans from your credit file forever!"

Do yourself a favor and save some money, too. Don't believe these statements. Only time, a conscious effort, and a personal debt repayment plan will improve your credit report. This brochure explains how you can improve your creditworthiness and gives legitimate resources for low or no-cost help.

The Scam

Everyday, companies nationwide appeal to consumers with poor credit histories. They promise, for a fee, to clean up your credit report so you can get a car loan, a home mortgage, insurance, or even a job. The truth is, they can't deliver. After you pay them hundreds or thousands of dollars in fees, these companies do nothing to improve your credit report; most simply vanish with your money.

The Warning Signs

If you decide to respond to a credit repair offer, look for these tell-tale signs of a scam:

- companies that want you to pay for credit repair services before they provide any services.

- companies that do not tell you your legal rights and what you can do for yourself for free.

- companies that recommend that you not contact a credit reporting company directly.

- companies that suggest that you try to invent a "new" credit identity — and then, a new credit report — by applying for an Employer Identification Number to use instead of your Social Security number.

- companies that advise you to dispute all information in your credit report or take any action that seems illegal, like creating a new credit identity. If you follow illegal advice and commit fraud, you may be subject to prosecution.

You could be charged and prosecuted for mail or wire fraud if you use the mail or telephone to apply for credit and provide false information. It's a federal crime to lie on a loan or credit application, to misrepresent your Social Security number, and to obtain an Employer Identification Number from the Internal Revenue Service under false pretenses.
Under the Credit Repair Organizations Act, credit repair companies cannot require you to pay until they have completed the services they have promised.

The Truth

No one can legally remove accurate and timely negative information from a credit report. The law allows you to ask for an investigation of information in your file that you dispute as inaccurate or incomplete. There is no charge for this. Everything a credit repair clinic can do for you legally, you can do for yourself at little or no cost. According to the Fair Credit Reporting Act (FCRA):

- You're entitled to a free report if a company takes adverse action against you, like denying your application for credit, insurance, or employment, and you ask for your report within 60 days of receiving notice of the action. The notice will give you the name, address, and phone number of the consumer reporting company. You're also entitled to one free report a year if you're unemployed and plan to look for a job within 60 days; if you're on welfare; or if your report is inaccurate because of fraud, including identity theft.

- Each of the nationwide consumer reporting companies — Equifax, Experian, and TransUnion — is required to provide you with a free copy of your credit report, at your request, once every 12 months.
  The three companies have set up a central website, a toll-free telephone number, and a mailing address through which you can order your free annual report. To order, click on annualcreditreport.com, call 1-877-322-8228, or complete the Annual Credit Report Request Form and mail it to: Annual Credit Report Request Service, P.O. Box 105281, Atlanta, GA 30348-5281. You can print the form from ftc.gov/credit. Do not contact the three nationwide consumer reporting companies individually.

They are providing free annual credit reports only through annualcreditreport.com, 1-877-322-8228, and Annual Credit Report Request Service, P.O. Box 105281, Atlanta, GA 30348-5281. You may order your reports from each of the three nationwide consumer reporting companies at the same time, or you can order your report from each of the companies one at a time. For more information, see Your Access to Free Credit Reports at ftc.gov/credit.

Otherwise, a consumer reporting company may charge you up to $9.50 for another copy of your report within a 12-month period.

- You can dispute mistakes or outdated items for free. Under the FCRA, both the consumer reporting company and the information provider (that is, the person, company, or organization that provides information about you to a consumer reporting company) are responsible for correcting inaccurate or incomplete information in your report. To take advantage of all your rights under this law, contact the consumer reporting company and the information provider.

STEP ONE

Tell the consumer reporting company, in writing, what information you think is inaccurate. Include copies (NOT originals) of documents that support your position. In addition to providing your complete name and address, your letter should clearly identify each item in your report you dispute, state the facts and explain why you dispute the information, and request that it be removed or corrected. You may want to enclose a copy of your report with the items in question circled. Your letter may look something like the one on page 6.

Send your letter by certified mail, "return receipt requested," so you can document what the consumer reporting company received. Keep copies of your dispute letter and enclosures.

Consumer reporting companies must investigate the items in question — usually within 30 days — unless they consider your dispute frivolous. They also must forward all the relevant data you provide about the inaccuracy to the organization that provided the information. After the information provider receives notice of a dispute from the consumer reporting company, it must investigate, review the relevant information, and report the results back to the consumer reporting company. If the information provider finds the disputed information is inaccurate, it must notify all three nationwide consumer reporting companies so they can correct the information in your file.

When the investigation is complete, the consumer reporting company must give you the results in writing and a free copy of your report if the dispute results in a change. If an item is changed or deleted, the consumer reporting company cannot put the disputed information back in your file unless the information provider verifies that it is accurate and complete. The consumer report in company also must send you written notice that includes the name, address, and phone number of the information provider. If you request, the consumer reporting company must send notices of any correction to anyone who received your report in the past six months. You can have a corrected copy of your report sent to anyone who received a copy during the past two years for employment purposes.

If an investigation doesn't resolve your dispute with the consumer reporting company, you can ask that a statement of the dispute be included in your file and in future reports. You also can ask the consumer reporting company to provide your statement to anyone who received a copy of your report in the recent past. You can expect to pay a fee for this service.

STEP TWO

Tell the creditor or other information provider, in writing, that you dispute an item. Be sure to include copies (NOT originals) of documents that support your position. Many providers specify an address for disputes. If the provider reports the item to a consumer reporting company, it must include a notice of your dispute. And if you are correct – that is, if the information is found to be inaccurate – the information provider may not report it again.

For more information, see How to Dispute Credit Report Errors at ftc.gov/credit.

Reporting Accurate Negative Information

When negative information in your report is accurate, only the passage of time can assure its removal. A consumer reporting company can report most accurate negative information for seven years and bankruptcy information for 10 years. Information about an unpaid judgment against you can be reported for seven years or until the statute of limitations runs out, whichever is longer. There is no time limit on reporting: information about criminal convictions; information reported in response to your application for a job that pays more than $75,000 a year; and information reported because you've applied for more than $150,000 worth of credit or life insurance. There is a standard method for calculating the seven-year reporting period. Generally, the period runs from the date that the event took place.

For more information, see Building a Better Credit Report at ftc.gov/credit.

The Credit Repair Organizations Act

By law, credit repair organizations must give you a copy of the "Consumer Credit File Rights Under State and Federal Law" before you sign a contract. They also must give you a written contract that spells out your rights and obligations. Read these documents before you sign anything. The law contains specific protections for you. For example, a credit repair company cannot:

- make false claims about their services
- charge you until they have completed the promised services
- perform any services until they have your signature on a written contract and have completed a three-day waiting period. During this time, you can cancel the contract without paying any fees

Your contract must specify:

- the payment terms for services, including their total cost
- a detailed description of the services to be performed
- how long it will take to achieve the results
- any guarantees they offer
- the company's name and business address

Have You Been Victimized?

Many states have laws regulating credit repair companies. State law enforcement officials may be helpful if you've lost money to credit repair scams.

If you've had a problem with a credit repair company, don't be embarrassed to report it. While you may fear that contacting the government will only make your problems worse, remember that laws are in place to protect you. Contact your local consumer affairs office or your state Attorney General (AGs). Many AGs have toll-free consumer hotlines. Check the Blue Pages of your telephone directory for the phone number or check www.naag.org for a list of state Attorneys General.

Need Help? Don't Despair

Just because you have a poor credit report doesn't mean you won't be able to get credit. Creditors set their own credit-granting standards and not all of them look at your credit history the same way. Some may look only at more recent years to evaluate you for credit, and they may grant credit if your bill-paying history has improved. It may be worthwhile to contact creditors informally to discuss their credit standards.

If you're not disciplined enough to create a workable budget and stick to it, work out a repayment plan with your creditors, or keep track of mounting bills, consider contacting a credit counseling organization. Many credit counseling organizations are nonprofit and work with you to solve your financial problems. But not all are reputable. For example, just because an organization says it's "nonprofit," there's no guarantee that its services are free, affordable, or even legitimate. In fact, some credit counseling organizations charge high fees, or hide their fees by pressuring consumers to make "voluntary" contributions that only cause more debt.

Most credit counselors offer services through local offices, the Internet, or on the telephone. If possible, find an organization that offers in-person counseling. Many universities, military bases, credit unions, housing authorities, and branches of the U.S. Cooperative Extension Service operate nonprofit credit counseling programs. Your financial institution, local consumer protection agency, and friends and family also may be good sources of information and referrals.

If you are considering filing for bankruptcy, you should know about one major change to the bankruptcy laws: As of October 17, 2005, you must get credit counseling from a government-approved organization within six months before you file for bankruptcy relief. You can find a state-by-state list of government-approved organizations at www.usdoj.gov/ust. That is the website of the U.S. Trustee Program, the organization within the U.S. Department of Justice that supervises bankruptcy cases and trustees.

Reputable credit counseling organizations can advise you on managing your money and debts, help you develop a budget, and offer free educational materials and workshops. Their counselors are certified and trained in the areas of consumer credit, money and debt management, and budgeting. Counselors discuss your entire financial situation with you, and help you develop a personalized plan to solve your money problems. An initial counseling session typically lasts an hour, with an offer of follow-up sessions.

For more information, see Knee Deep in Debt and Fiscal Fitness: Choosing a Credit Counselor at ftc.gov/credit.

Do-It-Yourself Check-Up

Even if you don't have a poor credit history, some financial advisors and consumer advocates suggest you review your credit report periodically

- because the information it contains affects whether you can get a loan or insurance — and how much you will have to pay for it.

- to make sure the information is accurate, complete, and up-to-date before you apply for a loan for a major purchase like a house or car, buy insurance, or apply for a job.

- to help guard against identity theft. That's when someone uses your personal information — like your name, your Social Security number, or your credit card number — to commit fraud. Identity thieves may use your information to open a new credit card account in your name. Then, when they don't pay the bills, the delinquent account is reported on your credit report. Inaccurate information like that could affect your ability to get credit, insurance, or even a job.

The FTC works for the consumer to prevent fraudulent, deceptive, and unfair business practices in the marketplace and to provide information to help consumers spot, stop, and avoid them. To file a complaint or to get free information on consumer issues, visit ftc.gov or call toll-free, 1-877-FTC-HELP (1-877-382-4357); TTY: 1-866-653-4261. The FTC enters consumer complaints into the Consumer Sentinel Network, a secure online database and investigative tool used by hundreds of civil and criminal law enforcement agencies in the U.S. and abroad.

Sample Dispute Letter for Credit Disputes

Date
Your Name
Your Address
Your City, State, Zip Code

Complaint Department
Name of Company
Address
City, State, Zip Code

Dear Sir or Madam:

I am writing to dispute the following information in my file. The items I dispute also are encircled on the attached copy of the report I received.

This item (identify item(s) disputed by name of source, such as creditors or tax court, and identify type of item, such as credit account, judgment, etc.) is (inaccurate or incomplete) because (describe what is inaccurate or incomplete and why). I am requesting that the item be deleted (or request another specific change) to correct the information.

Enclosed are copies of (use this sentence if applicable and describe any enclosed documentation, such as payment records, court documents) supporting my position. Please investigate this (these) matter(s) and (delete or correct) the disputed item(s) as soon as possible.

Sincerely,
Your name

Enclosures: (List what you are enclosing)

Simple and Compound Interest

What I want to show you now is the power of simple and compound interest.

Simple interest is money that a financial institution pays you for the use of your money at a certain interest rate. It is paid based on a fixed number of days at a fixed rate (usually).

Compound interest is money that a financial institution pays you that is added daily, monthly, quarterly or annually depending on the terms of the agreement. It is based on the balance that you in your account each day.

The flip side of this is where you owe money to a financial institution. If you are paying credit card payments or on a mortgage, the chances are that you are paying simple or compound interest.

This works for banks, insurance companies and business. It can and will work for you just as easily. The secret is:

1. Make consistent contributions to your savings.
2. Don't touch the money.
3. If you can, increase the amount of your savings to account for inflation. Don't sweat it if you can't though. As far as I am concerned, savings is savings.

Your biggest killers of savings are:

Not making consistent savings.

When you are withdrawing from savings when you really shouldn't.

Not factoring in for inflation.

Please try to save some money from each paycheck each week. For years, financial advisors have stated to save at least 10%

of your paycheck. I suggest you save as much as you can. Studies have indicated that most people will not have enough money in case of a catastrophic financial emergency or they will run out of money when they retire.

If you can, in addition to you saving money, please teach your children the importance of savings. You will thank yourself as your children grow up to be financially independent. As a friend of mine, Deborah Simpson says, "If your children grow up to be happy and financially independent, you will be happy as well."

When money is borrowed, interest is charged for the use of that money for a certain period of time. When the money is paid back, the principal (amount of money that was borrowed) and the interest is paid back. The amount to interest depends on the interest rate, the amount of money borrowed (principal) and the length of time that the money is borrowed.

The formula for finding simple interest is:

*Interest = Principal * Rate * Time.*

If $100 was borrowed for 2 years at a 10% interest rate, the interest would be $100*10/100*2 = $20.

The total amount that would be due would be
$100+$20=$120.
Simple interest is generally charged for borrowing money for short periods of time.

Compound interest is similar but the total amount due at the end of each period is calculated and further interest is charged against both the original principal but also the interest that was earned during that period.

It is the accumulation of interest that either makes investments wonderful over time or makes your life miserable if you are paying off credit cards or loans over time and not making anything more than the minimum payment.

Learn the power of simple and compound interest!

Initial Investment = $10,000

Time (Years)	Rate of Growth					
	5%	6%	10%	11%	15%	20%
5	12,763	13,382	16,105	16,851	20,114	24,883
10	16,289	17,908	25,937	28,394	40,456	61,917
15	20,789	23,966	41,772	47,846	81,371	154,070
20	26,533	32,071	67,275	80,623	163,665	383,376
25	33,864	42,919	108,347	135,855	329,190	953,962
30	43,219	57,435	174,494	228,923	662,118	2,373,763
35	55,160	76,861	281,024	385,749	1,331,755	5,906,682
40	70,400	102,857	452,593	650,009	2,678,635	14,697,716

What Ten Thousand Dollars Can Do If It Can Stay Put and Grow

Here is a table of how $10,000 of your money can grow if you actually save it. Even at 5% for forty years you are looking at having $70,400 for the money just staying put.

If inflation kicks in deeper, it would not be unusual to see interest rates jump back up to 15 or 20%

Of course, the cost of goods would go up and you would probably be spending $100 for a salad and $50 for a cup of coffee.

A sobering note to close the topic on is that even taking inflation into account, it is a good idea to have money in a savings account.

Yes, you can lose money to inflation but you still will be better off than the people who have no savings. If you are in a financial crunch, you want to have cash to pay the bills!

Long Term Investments

Your long term investments are stocks, bonds, mutual funds, savings accounts, precious metals, or investment properties that you will be buying and holding onto.

Look and watch – don't touch.

Pay attention to what the investments are doing but be patient. Investments tend to go in cycles and sometimes cycles just sit there and stagnate. If you respond with knee jerk reactions, that can cost you a lot of money.

To prevent having all your eggs in one financial basket and similar to what we were talking about in the retirement chapter, you want to make sure that you will be able to stomach any changes in the financial markets till you hit your retirement. The money that you are investing for the long term should be monitored but be very cautious about reallocating assets. It is very hard if not impossible to try to "time" the markets and investing.

It makes financial sense to diversify. That means to take your money and place it into three separate funds or types of investments for the long term.

The first type of investment would be for a guaranteed interest rate of some kind. You will know that you will be making a fixed rate of money after a certain period of time. You potentially will lose money due to inflation but the trade off will be you will be guaranteed to have the money there when you retire (providing the place where you have invested your money with is still in business).

Consult with financial advisors that you can trust. Make sure that you are doing whatever you can be doing now to saving your money because despite everybody's best intentions, nobody knows what the future will bring.

Account for Taxes

Almost every tax season I end up with clients who have made what you or I would call a good living and end up owing money to the Fed or the State of California. What basically happens is that a person gets a windfall profit:

1. They sold a screenplay or some product.
2. They won a cash prize or lottery ticket.
3. Their business picked up and all of a sudden there is a demand for their contractual services.
4. They got a bonus and they didn't have enough taxes taken out.

Somewhere along the line, they ended up spending most of the money they received. They forget that they had to put aside money for taxes. When April rolls around next year it generally is too late.

If you are a resident of the United States, you should know that we are in a "pay as you go" tax program as of the printing of this book. That means that you are required to pay taxes to the Federal government when you receive any worldwide income.

Most states follow the Federal government if they have a state income tax.

That means that you are expected to pay estimated taxes as close as you can to when you received the money.

You can make quarterly tax payments and more information can be found from the IRS website here:

http://search.irs.gov/web/query.html?col=allirs&charset=utf-8&qp=&qs=-Wct%3A%22Internal+Revenue+Manual%22&qc=&qm=0&rf=0&oq=&qt=1040+ES

That particular search is a general one and you need to make sure you get the 1040 ES form for the year that you are making estimated tax payments for. For example if you are making money in Jan 2008, you will need to pay the estimated payments and file a 1040-ES for 2008 by April 15, 2008.

For respective states information, please visit:

http://www.kimgreenblatt.com/hsfcp/statetax.htm

You can also look on a search engine for the specific state and income tax.

A general rule of thumb is to put aside at least a third of any income you receive aside.

If you live in a state that has state income taxes, the one third of your income received for taxes should cover that amount as well.

If you already owe the IRS or state agencies money or have underpaid, you will have to either pay more in estimated payments or expect to owe money and possibly get an underpayment penalty when you file taxes next year. Please do your own due diligence and research to make sure that you are not going to penalized.

The penalties for underpayment of taxes can be severe but the bigger issue is that if you don't put the money aside that might indicate you are sloppy with saving for tax payments elsewhere in your finances!

So, let us say that you won a small slot machine jackpot of $10,000 on a Native American reservation where slot machines are legal.

If you live in California here is how the scenario might play out. The casino will give you a W-2G and you may be able to have money withheld for Federal taxes, maybe not for State taxes. A lot of time no money is withheld and that is the problem.

Here is how the money would breakdown in the form of payments:

Out of the $10,000, put aside a third of the winnings ($3,330 or so) and out of that make sure you either have withheld for the Fed 2/3 of your money or are will send it in as a check or direct electronic debit to the Fed before the next quarterly due date.

For more information on Federal tax due dates, please visit www.irs.gov.

So, what is 2/3 of $3,330? That is $2,220.
The remaining $1,110 would be paid as the estimated payment for your respective state. If you live in a state without state tax, good for you!

You still will have $6,670. Congratulations and use it wisely!

So, let us say that you sold a lot of widgets you made at home in the month of May 2008 and made $5000 and you lived in California.

You have a deadline for quarterly estimated taxes of June 15, 2008 and you would want to send in:

$5000
X   .33 (1/3)
_____
$1650

Out of that you want to take 2/3 of this which is $1650 x .67 = $1105.50 so round it up to $1106 for your June estimated payment to the Fed and the remaining $544 for the Franchise Tax Board for the State of California.

Again, these are just estimates but they should cut down on most problems you will encounter if you find yourselves getting extra cash during the year.

Just remember that you will be taxed on it and it is better to pay the taxes now than later (in my opinion).

While we are at it, please start teaching your kids now about taxes. Tax planning is not covered in schools. It should be. Talk with your teachers and instructors.

If they aren't interested, be a hero and start teaching them now that even though taxes are boring and the butt of a lot of jokes (they will laugh if you use the word "butt") they are part of life and need to be dealt with.

Let's now talk about taxes and whether you should work at home or out of the house.

Work At Home or Work Away From Home and some Taxing Questions

Competition is fierce for stay at home jobs. More and more people, especially parents with young children, are trying to find gigs where they can work from home. Everybody talks about computer sales, service from home and things like that. The reality is if you are going to be working from home you need to carry yourself as a professional.

Let's say that you are working as a call center representative from home. That means that you need to have your own room in your house or apartment. There should be no crying babies or screaming kids nearby. You will be expected to make or take phone calls and do whatever it is you need to do. If it is a financial services company, you need to be focused on the details of your customer's questions.

No distractions.

If you are taking calls for pizzas for delivery, you need to be able to follow whatever script is given to you for suggestive selling food, delivery instructions, etc. Expect to be called by in-house mystery shoppers to see what kind of service you are giving or to be subjected to a lot of feedback from people who call in for the customer service.

Customer service jobs from home may sound great but you need to be able to be disciplined enough to work without having to deal with family distractions. The kids and your spouse need to know that Mom or Dad is working when you close the door to the office or through the blanket on the doorway.

Some people want to get part time sales jobs outside of the house because they know that if they are home that they will have to deal with family distractions. For stay at home Moms or Dads, it is also a great way to get out into the world. Psychologically, it may be the only connection to the adult world that these people are getting and it is a great way to maintain one's sanity.

What is my personal opinion?

It depends on what you want. I telecommute and work outside of the house. I am very disciplined and the people in the house know that if I am working, unless a giant space squid is attacking the house, I am not to be disturbed. I make sure that if it is an emergency that they can get to me with signs or if it is a *real* emergency and Mom can't handle it or she is out, they scream, "Dad, come quickly."

Since I am not on the phone doing customer service calls that isn't a problem. I can still hear what is going on.

If I really need to concentrate on something, for example, if I am writing or editing a book, I sometimes go to the public library. I make sure that my Internet access is disabled.

That brings up another important point. No Internet surfing while you are working from your home computer. You are there to work and not surf. If you are also serious about working using your computer, I strongly suggest that you get a stripped down laptop or standalone computer to be used dedicated for work.

If you get an audit-from-hell (rare though it may happen) from the Internal Revenue Service or your state tax authority, you want to be able to demonstrate that you are treating your part time job as real work. Having a dedicated business computer goes a long way to showing that you aren't playing games.

Since I have started talking about the tax ramifications I need to make you aware (or remind you if you already knew) about business expenses. If you are working for somebody, you can take employee business expenses if they are not reimbursed. If you are treated as a contractor, you may be able to deduct 100% of certain expenses.

How will you know the difference?

1. Save all your receipts for starters. You won't be able to start making distinctions until you know what your expenses are. The IRS also wants to have proof for anything that you may end up claiming as a deduction or expense.

2. Start learning how to research the IRS website or if you don't have the desire, find a good tax person you can trust.

   The IRS website, www.irs.gov, has a lot of information on how to file taxes. Important documents you should research on are Schedule A, Form 2106, Schedule C. Make sure if you are searching on the forms that you find them for the appropriate year that you are filing. In other words, if you are filing your 2007 taxes you want the Form 2106 for 2007. Please pay attention to the details.

   Schedule A is for itemized deductions. Form 2106 is Employee Business Expenses. Schedule C is Form 1040, Profit or Loss from Business. You generally use Form 2106 if you are an employee. You generally use Schedule C if you are treated as self-employed.

   If you will be receiving a W-2, you are treated at the end of the year as an employee. If the company will be giving you 1099 at the end of the year, you are treated as a contractor or self-employed.

On the IRS website you can also find the instructions for completing these forms. It would be a good idea for you to familiarize yourself with the forms. They contain a lot of information as to what can be claimed and the proper place to put it on the forms. It is important that you have the forms filled out correctly because they tend to be audited because of people trying to pull fast ones and just doing the forms incorrectly.

Again, if there are any questions, please consult with a tax professional.

To paraphrase from the IRS website on business expenses if you are **self-employed**:

Business Expenses

Business expenses are the cost of carrying on a trade or business. These expenses are usually deductible if the business is operated to make a profit.

What Can I Deduct?

To be deductible, a business expense must be both ordinary and necessary. An ordinary expense is one that is common and accepted in your trade or business. A necessary expense is one that is helpful and appropriate for your trade or business. An expense does not have to be indispensable to be considered necessary.

It is important to separate business expenses from the following expenses:

The expenses used to figure the cost of goods sold,
Capital Expenses, and
Personal Expenses.
Cost of Goods Sold

If your business manufactures products or purchases them for resale, you generally must value inventory at the beginning and end of each tax year to determine your cost of goods sold. Some of your expenses may be included in figuring the cost of goods sold. Cost of goods sold is deducted from your gross receipts to figure your gross profit for the year. If you include an expense in the cost of goods sold, you cannot deduct it again as a business expense.

The following are types of expenses that go into figuring the cost of goods sold.

The cost of products or raw materials, including freight
Storage
Direct labor costs (including contributions to pensions or annuity plans) for workers who produce the products
Factory overhead
Under the uniform capitalization rules, you must capitalize the direct costs and part of the indirect costs for certain production or resale activities. Indirect costs include rent, interest, taxes, storage, purchasing, processing, repackaging, handling, and administrative costs.

This rule does not apply to personal property you acquire for resale if your average annual gross receipts (or those of your predecessor) for the preceding 3 tax years are not more than $10 million.

For additional information, refer to the chapter on Cost of goods sold, Publication 334, Tax Guide for Small Businesses and the chapter on Inventories, Publication 538, Accounting Periods and Methods from the IRS website.

Capital Expenses

You must capitalize, rather than deduct, some costs. These costs are a part of your investment in your business and are called capital expenses. Capital expenses are considered assets in your business. There are, in general, three types of costs you capitalize.

Business start-up cost (See the note below)
Business assets
Improvements
Note: You can elect to deduct or amortize certain business start-up costs. Refer to chapters 7 and 8 of Publication 535, Business Expenses.

Personal versus Business Expenses

Generally, you cannot deduct personal, living, or family expenses. However, if you have an expense for something that is used partly for business and partly for personal purposes, divide the total cost between the business and personal parts. You can deduct the business part.

For example, if you borrow money and use 70% of it for business and the other 30% for a family vacation, you can deduct 70% of the interest as a business expense. The remaining 30% is personal interest and is not deductible. Refer to chapter 4 of Publication 535, Business Expenses, for information on deducting interest and the allocation rules.

Business Use of Your Home

If you use part of your home for business, you may be able to deduct expenses for the business use of your home. These expenses may include mortgage interest, insurance, utilities, repairs, and depreciation. Refer to Publication 587, Business Use of Your Home, for more information.

Business Use of Your Car

If you use your car in your business, you can deduct car expenses. If you use your car for both business and *personal purposes, you must divide your expenses based on actual mileage. Refer to Publication 463, Travel, Entertainment, Gift, and Car Expenses. For a list of current and prior year mileage rates see the Standard Mileage Rates.*

Other Types of Business Expenses

Employees' Pay - You can generally deduct the pay you give your employees for the services they perform for your business.

Retirement Plans - Retirement plans are savings plans that offer you tax advantages to set aside money for your own, and your employees' retirement.

Rent Expense - Rent is any amount you pay for the use of property you do not own. In general, you can deduct rent as an expense only if the rent is for property you use in your trade or business. If you have or will receive equity in or title to the property, the rent is not deductible.

Interest - Business interest expense is an amount charged for the use of money you borrowed for business activities.

Taxes - You can deduct various federal, state, local, and foreign taxes directly attributable to your trade or business as business expenses.

Insurance - Generally, you can deduct the ordinary and necessary cost of insurance as a business expense, if it is for your trade, business, or profession.

This list is not all inclusive of the types of business expenses that you can deduct. For additional information, refer to Publication 535, Business Expenses.

Okay, you can see that it covers a lot of ground and that is just the tip of the iceberg. You are starting to get the idea.

What about if you are an employee and **WORK for SOMEBODY ELSE?**

The forms that you will want to research as well as the supporting tax instructions are:

Form 1040 Schedule A – Itemized Deductions

Form 2106 or Form 2106-EZ as mentioned before is Employee Business Expenses

Publication 463 - Travel, Entertainment, Gift, and Car Expenses
Business entertainment expenses and business gift expenses may be deductible, but subject to certain limits.

Publication 1542 Per Diem Rates – If you travel the United States and are not reimbursed for meals and lodging, you need to check out what the IRS allows for each city.

Publication 529 – Miscellaneous Deductions

These are just to get you started.

You also need to find out or determine from your employer if you are working under what is called an "accountable plan". Check with your Human Resources department to find out.

If your employer reimbursed you or gave you an advance or allowance for your employee business expenses that is treated as paid under an accountable plan, the payment should not be shown on your Form W-2 as pay. You do not include the payment in your income.

To be an accountable plan, your employer's reimbursement or allowance arrangement must include all three of the following rules:

You must have paid or incurred expenses that are deductible while performing services as an employee.
You must adequately account to your employer for these expenses within a reasonable time period, and
You must return any excess reimbursement or allowance within a reasonable time period.

If your employer's reimbursement arrangement does not meet all three requirements, the payments you receive should be included in the wages shown on your Form W–2. You must report the payments as income, and you must complete Form 2106 or Form 2106-EZ and itemize your deductions to deduct your expenses.

If you were reimbursed for travel or transportation under an accountable plan, but at a per diem or mileage rate that exceeds the Federal rate, the excess should be included in the wages on your Form W–2. If your actual expenses exceed the Federal rate, you must itemize your deductions to deduct the excess. For information about the Federal per diem rates, refer to Publication 1542 and for information regarding mileage rates refer to Publication 463.

Clear as mud, huh? Again, please consult your own tax person when making business decisions or due your own research. Each year tax law changes and it is important that you or your tax person know what you can or can't take as a deduction and plan for it accordingly.

As part of your decision whether to take a part time job or not, as I mentioned in another chapter, please take a look at what your transportation costs would be to work the part time job. Gasoline prices have somewhat stabilized as of the printing of this book. That being said, they are not cheap and if you are shelling out anywhere upwards of $3 a gallon for gas, you will need to factor that in when making a decision to drive 20 miles to work. Hopefully the chapter you just read will get you thinking about what you need to do if you decide to work at home or away.

Reviving Our Dead Service Economy

Let's face it; the United States has fallen down in terms of being a service economy. You can do your part to help clean up our act as well as get and keep part time service oriented jobs by remembering to do some simple things.

When you are at work, focus on work. Have you ever been waiting in line at a cashier and you see that there is a co-worker who isn't on shift yet who is trying to flirt with the cashier? How about they are talking about their horrible night at Suzy's house? If they were working for me, they would get talked to and on the second offense they would be fired.

Make sure that if you are working a service job that you pay attention to the people who are in front of you. If there is downtime, there isn't a problem with minimal talking but if there are customers who are spending money, you need to take care of them.

How do you like it when you have to wait while people who don't care about what they are doing treat you like you are not worth their time? And they are getting paid for it....

Take the time to learn the products and services that you are selling. The customers are coming to you to get information about what you have. Sometimes you can get a little bit more out of sales by taking the time to answer their questions about the details of the different things that you sell.

Keep a smile on your face and be polite. I don't care if it is artificial or fake. It helps lighten the mood and grumpy customers will lighten up if you are trying to help them after they have been waiting in line.

Take the time to help people with special needs. Most places of employment pay lip service to helping special needs but they don't practice what they preach. If you see somebody in a wheelchair, offer to help if they are having a hard time carrying something or with opening a door.

Assume that if a person is talking or moving slowly that maybe that is just how they operate. Maybe they are high functioning autistic so be patient. The same holds true for children and elderly people.

Human beings don't move at Internet speed and from what I have experienced of most people who have been working in the service business these days they don't even move at melting glacier speed.

Take care of people the way that you want to be taken care of and things will go well for you, your business and your employer.

Safety issues are very important. If there is something that isn't safe in the work environment notify your boss and do what steps you can to fix it. Pay attention to your surroundings.

Come to work clean, well groomed and cover any tats that you have on your arms if you are working in a conservative environment. The one exception is if you are working in a conservative tattoo parlor. In that case, wear short sleeves so people can see your art. If you are working in a trendy store where your body art and facial piercing can be worn, be judicious about it. Your Human Resources people or boss will tell you what you can or can't do but take the time to listen and act on what he or she tells you so you don't get fired your first week!

All that information is just common sense but since they don't seem to be teaching common sense in school anymore I felt it had to be said and my apologies if you already are practicing good customer service skills!

Do What You Love, But Don't Let It Destroy You Financially

I use to love reading comic books. When I got into the comic business, I was very fortunate because I had talked to a lot of comic store owners and they kept me from going nuts. I had previous experience in other ventures and I approached the comic delivery service as a business.

At the time, other fan boys like me got into the business and went broke. They went nuts ordering all sorts of products like pogs, statues, books that they liked and they thought other people would like.

The same goes for you if you are into selling Avon or anything that you already order. You don't want to turn into your own best customer. Stick to what your customers want and watch your profit margins.

I have said this before but it bears repeating:

NOBODY EVER WENT BROKE SELLING OUT ALL OF THEIR INVENTORY

If you under order something and it turns out to be the hottest thing on the planet, great. You will have sold it all out and made some money. If you can reorder the product, watch your orders so you don't end up stuck with inventory you can't sell. Just order what you think you can sell and MAYBE a little extra.

Personally, after having been burnt so many times, I would only order enough to sell through to all my customers. All it takes is one "over order" that is enough to sting you financially to make you want to tighten your cost controls.

Retirement

You need to start planning your retirement early. By that I mean there is no time that is too early to start saving money, thinking about what kind of lifestyle you want to live in and thinking about how you are going to survive.

Years ago I received some advice from a friend who said I was too young to start worrying about my "sunset" years. That may have been true only to a point. If you are aware that the good times (and bad) may not last forever you can save during the good times so you can have during the bad.

If you are already retired, you need to do what you can to hang onto your money for the roller coaster ride that is ahead of us. For the immediate future, because of the international nature of commerce, there is no clear picture anymore of how things will be.

The expression "Past performance does not guarantee future returns" really hits home in this era.

Contact financial planners, use the internet and for goodness sake save money where you can. It is a lot easier for people who have money to start with to make money than those of us who don't.

Even though our current work market may not be called a recession, if you have lost your job, your home and are almost out of your mind, it is a recession if not a depression for you.

Please seek out somebody to talk to counseling and for financial advice.

Money Is Tight and It Is About To Get Tighter

As I come to toward s the end of the book I have to point out that across the United States, people who have had home equity lines and who have had good credit are finding that their lines of credit are being frozen.

People are losing their jobs because we are still reeling from bad financial decisions by people in banking, in politics and let's face it, ourselves.

We have gotten so use to living in credit world that we did not stop to remember the fine print. The home equity lines were basically that, extensions of credit from the bank and not your money to keep.

The next market correction I expect to see will be tightening of credit cards. The people who will be clobbered the most will be people who are living from check to check and are using their credit cards as income.

I have been harping on savings and paying off debt as part of your money making survival skills.

Take some time now and make a list of your assets – the items that you own free and clear and your liabilities. Everything that you owe money and take some time to see what can you eliminate from your monthly budget.

The cliché is that "Tough times don't last, but tough people do."

The handwriting is on the wall for financial well being and the immediate future is an interesting mix and mess of low salary wages, high inflation and tight credit. I already said that the best thing we can do is start working on our infrastructure in this country.

With more Midwestern flooding, it is clear that the insurance industry is not going to have the money to bail out the homes that are constantly piling up as debris from natural disasters.

Protect yourself, dear reader. The fact that you are taking the time to read this and financially work at surviving the problems that we are facing means that you are going to make it.

When you are shopping for goods and services, do what you can to use coupons or discounts. That will help you save money and if you owe money, throw the savings towards reducing the mortgage payment or the credit card debt that seems to be creeping up.

If you have a variable rate loan, for the next few years, as of the printing of this book, I suspect the Federal Reserve will try to leave the interest rates alone because they frankly are stuck between inflation and everybody going broke at once. Take advantage of this to pay off the other debts if there is higher interest all the time watching the interest rates.

Read and re-read any financial contracts and statements that you have on your mortgages, lines of credit, home equity loans, and credit cards. Look for what they can do to freeze your money or charge you extra for interest rates.

These are sobering times and the best way to deal with this is to keep your sense of humor and optimism while being realistic. As I stated in the preface to this book, everybody is in the same boat. People who are over-extended in their McMansions are just as bad as people who are over-extended in their townhouses. The problems are reversible; it starts with learning how to rethink how we do things.

A few generations ago the United States had a depression of epic proportions. The difference this time is that it is coming in waves of lingering damage instead of all at once.

Current estimates are between two to four years till property values level off and start to rise.

That means that for you, if you have any business ideas that would work during a depression you can make money.

As a publisher, I feel that books (like this one) that can help people save money are great. Books on how to do things such as self-help for repairing furniture, etc, will sell well.

Books, movies and music that deal with spirituality, religion and anything with fantasy sell well in a depressed economy. People want to escape, at least for a few hours mentally, from their daily lives. They want their entertainment as well and they will pay for it.

In my case, I have found that people also will turn towards gambling as a "last chance to make it big". Lottery sales hit new highs despite being a horrible gamble. The odds of hitting the lottery are almost the same whether you play or don't. Despite the fact that I hate poker, I am good at it and have written some books on poker and they have sold.

I do like craps or dice and I ended up writing a book on dice. It has sold well and that leads me to believe that there is going to be more interest in other gambling books, novelties, etc other than poker since poker is pretty much played out in the media. People still go to card clubs but the poker book sales have flattened.

I think there will always be a market for the "next big thing". I am sadly not one who has any clue as to what the "next big thing" is but as I stated elsewhere in the book and on my blog (information about that is available at the end of the book), the key items that people look for are:

1. Time Saving
2. Novelty
3. A Coolness Factor
4. Multiple Features

If a product can save people time, they will spend all sorts of money on it. Take GPS mapping systems. People love the fact that they can jump into the car, plot the course to whatever place they want without having to write anything down. They pay between $80-800 for the units not including subscriptions to local traffic. Personally, I would just map my trip before leaving the house and listen to the radio for traffic news but I am all about saving money, not spending it. You can see how large the GPS systems are.

They save time, they have moved from novelty to necessity (or perceived one at any rate) for some people, they are "cool" and some models allow you to play music, synch with your phone, etc.

If you can hit the mark taking an existing product and engineering it so that people will want to use it or perceive that they have to have it, they will buy it regardless of the state of the economy.

Look for niche products or markets that haven't been mined to death or talked about on the internet. That will be the key to getting something that you can make money off of in the coming economic belt tightening.

Invest in some prototypes. If you think you have an idea for the next big inexpensive item, see if you can build a sample one or work with an engineer who can design a sample for you. It will also help you get funding.

With tight money and tight times in the United States will come people with money from other countries.

Welcome them, they will come with their Euros, Yuan, and whatever else that may have a better rate of exchange than the dollar and they will invest and do business here.

Take the time to learn some other languages. If you know Spanish, Chinese, French, Japanese or Italian, you are ahead of the game.

If you can adapt to change, you will thrive. Whether you believe in evolution or not, the way of the business world is that you need to be flexible and change. If you can do that, you will make money, survive a recession, a layoff and any credit problems that you have!

Three Awesome Closing Bits of Advice

Stay Profitable

If you are making money in what you are doing but unhappy, that is okay. Take whatever steps you need to do for trying to change your vocation. Whatever you do please don't stop what you are doing if you are turning a profit. People don't get it that sometimes they have a knack for something that they don't like to do and should be doing it.

Don't Go Into Business To Lose Money

Make sure that you have a rock solid business plan. You aren't going to be going into business to lose money. If it looks like in your business plan that you aren't going to be turning a profit you will need to revisit it two or three more times and then rework the numbers. You should then rethink why you would want to go into a business to lose money.

If you are in the business and losing money, look at what you can realistically do to change things or get out of business.

Mind Set Change From Spending To Savings

Look for anything you can to save money. Remember to practice ecologically sound saving ideas with your pocketbook first. Protect your financial environment!
If there is anything you can do to keep costs down, do it. As long as you aren't sacrificing something that is inherently part of your business, cut the cost.

I hope you have gotten at least one bit of information, suggestion or glimmer of wisdom from the book. These are trying times for all of us and it is important that we do what we can to protect our loved ones, our friends and ourselves. Good luck!
Interested in more information?

I can be found at http://www.kimgreenblatt.com

I can also be contacted at kimg@kimgreenblatt.com

The email address may change so check my website or blog for more information.

My blog, profitable, can be read at:

http://www.kimgreenblatt.com/wordpress

I write about business, gambling, poker, taxes, marketing, special needs and saving money. I also have a fiction line of books through Shockingly Awesome Press at:

http://www.shockinglyawesome.com

I look forward to helping you grow financially!

Part of the proceeds from the sales of this book goes to research for finding a cure for Rett Syndrome. Rett Syndrome affects one girl born on the planet every fifteen minutes. Boys with the Rett gene usually die at birth.

Good luck with your financial planning and you are in my thoughts and prayers!

www.ingramcontent.com/pod-product-compliance
Lightning Source LLC
Chambersburg PA
CBHW022158080426
42734CB00006B/490